ROCKPORT RECOLLECTED

Real Stories from Real People

by

ROGER MARTIN

THE CURIOUS TRAVELLER PRESS • GLOUCESTER, MASSACHUSETTS

Front Cover: *Miss Bradley's 1926 first and second grade class posed before the George J. Tarr school on School Street. The same building presently houses the Denghausen Library.*
PHOTO CREDIT: BETTY GRAHAM.

Back Cover: *An early 1920s view beneath the granite keystone bridge between Rockport and Pigeon Cove, looking into Flat Ledge quarry. Note in the far distance the derricks used to hoist the granite onto flat cars, hauled and transported over the rail tracks by the steam engine to Granite Pier, where it was then either cut into paving blocks or loaded directly on ocean going vessels to be taken all over the world.*
PHOTO CREDIT: DAVID KNOWLTON

DEDICATION

This book of local oral history is dedicated to Joseph, Gayla, Leah, Gregory, Jessica and Ronnie. And to Eleanor Hoy, who encouraged me to produce my books and put me in touch with David McAveeney, who published them.

Library of Congress Cataloging-in-Publication Data
Martin, Roger
Rockport Recollected—Real Stories from Real People
1st Edition
ISBN 1-892839-08-3

THE CURIOUS TRAVELLER PRESS
a division of
Thre Pressroom Printers, Incorporatred
32 Blackburn Center
Gloucester, Massachusetts

Contents

Author's Note

THIS SECOND CURIOUS TRAVELLER oral history features entirely different inter-views and photographs than those in *Rockport Remembered*. The photographs are for the most part from a personal Charles Cleaves collection of snapshots which his great niece, Betty Scatterday, has graciously given me permission to use for this book. Any non-Cleaves photographs will be so noted. The photographs are not meant to illustrate individual interviews, although there may be a few fortu-itous comparisons. They came to me without captions and I've attempted to note approximate locations but have, I'm sure, made more than my share of mistaken identities. The photographs are included to add visual substance to these per-sonal stories of other days, the intent being to present the reader with a pictori-al feel of what Rockport looked and felt like in many of the years recalled in these interviews.

As an aside here, I must admit to being a native Cape Anner when in the company of those few who happen to have been born in their living rooms or upstairs bedrooms on such and such a street in Rockport. To them I'm not a true Rockport native and never can be because my mother gave birth to me in the Addison Gilbert Hospital in Gloucester. I can understand the pride of this rapidly disappearing category of Rockport native but those of us who were born in the AGH do have one thing different from these "true" natives, we have birth certificates in both Gloucester and Rockport!

Although this book deals with one specific community, that of my home town Rockport, Massachusetts, it is my intent for these interviews and photo-graphs to be transferrable to many similar small towns which are experiencing the same disconnect from past values and moorings that accompanies the pres-ence of new, frequently very affluent citizens in their midst. For the most part this book features interviews with second generation Rockporters whose direct ancestors have come to this country from overseas and who have, by their dili-gence and hard work, laid much of the foundation of Rockport. These earlier immigrants were the people who added their sweat and toil to the tough and long-lasting aggregate that bound all Rockporters into the relatively homoge-neous community that I left in 1942 for military service.

Although there are some non-immigrant based stories in this collection, such as the excerpts from J. Raymond Smith's handwritten journal (presented with the kind permission of his son and grandson, Ray and Jay Smith) my main focus has been on what I think are the frequently forgotten people of Rockport, those notably Scandanavian, Italian and Irish people, many of whom were brought to town mainly as a source of cheap labor (for some record of this opin-ion see the interview with Gor Svenson and his description of meeting fellow

Swedes at the depot and they getting off the train, fresh from Immigration landings, with tags around their necks saying "To Rockport, Massachusetts, Rockport Granite Company").

The influx of newcomers into an area like ours, with a long local history of events and local characters, has from time to time produced inevitable frictions between those people who do undoubtedly love the town they have moved into just as much as those who have spent the major portion of their lives there. But the shared loves for a community between locals and newcomers have differing histories backing them up: the one enmeshed and enamored in and of local legends stretching back for generations and the other entranced by what the community has become much more recently, usually dating to post-World War II. After reading my first book of oral history, *Rockport Remembered*, some newcomers confided in me that they had not known that the town had been so "ethnic" not all that long ago. They were amazed that this had been so, just as I was amazed in turn that so many were unaware of those who went before them.

At the time of this publication Rockport has become gentrified as our national economy has blossomed and resulted in an incredible increase in the number of newcomers who understandably view our present look and ambiance as that which has always been here. It is my hope that these interviews with some people who can recall the often hardscrabble early days of Rockport will present a more complete and more realistic image of what and who preceded them here on the tip of the Cape. By presenting these insights into our earlier days I hope that our new neighbors will realize that what they see today is only a thin veneer over quite a different community.

Many long established towns such as Rockport have undergone major changes in their populations along with incredible demands upon formerly semi-abandoned fields, former woodlands and vacant shorefront properties. The resultant rise in prices for real estate has put terrible pressures on the descendants of these early immigrants. It has been a not uncommon experience in many desirable small communities to find sons and daughters of these immigrants priced out of the very communities for which their parents had so diligently labored as they literally built their adopted town.

World War II forced our involvement in affairs other than local for some few years. The increased mobility of the post-war years has also broadened our perceptions and experience of the world on the far side of the Annisquam. Many of today's nomadic generations seem unable to think about any form of history other than the time post-dating their own birth, heedlessly depriving themselves of any sense of place.

To be still living in the town of one's birth is marveled at by some, frequently accompanied by a dollop or two of barely hidden suspicion that there might be something missing in a person's character to have willingly spent ones life in just one place. It's no wonder that we seem to be losing a sense of national purpose in the insatiable rush to always be going somewhere else. Without the successful local there can be no national, and there are fewer and fewer such locals as ours to be found these days.

I wish to give my public thanks to David McAveeney for our writer-publisher relationship over the past few years. This is the third book of mine David has seen fit to put into print with no more than a nod and a handshake to set things in motion. Like so many references in the following interviews made to the way things were done in times past, this is a most satisfying way of doing business. I designed and carved at least five pipe shade systems for Charles Fisk at the C. B. Fisk pipe organ company following similar nods and handshakes. To have known and worked with and for two such people in one lifetime is more than anyone could have hoped for.

MARY BALZARINI ANDERSON

Born, 1907 on Curtis Street in Pigeon Cove. Mary is one of four surviving children of the 12 who were born to her mother. One little sister drowned but the eleven others survived to adulthood. There are two distinct Pigeon Cove Balzarini families, perhaps closely related way back, but probably distant cousins today. I lived only a block away from Mary and her family for over 30 years and we never spoke until I showed up to interview her for this book . . . such local anomalies were and are not uncommon to our town (or many other small New England towns). They frequently puzzle non-natives but we somehow have accepted these exceptions to what some think of as the norm and don't think much of most of them. Unfortunately Mary died before her interview was put into print.

MY FATHER ANTONE, and Charlie Balzarini, who had the family on Curtis Street, were the only two Balzarinis on the Cape in the early days. The two families were distantly related back in the Old Country. Both my mother and father came from the Old Country (Italy). My father came from a place where everything was a farm and he started a farm here. I had a cousin who went over across a few years ago and they said that the original farm is still there. During the war (World War II) the government took it over so they had to move out. But after the war they came back. So it's still being farmed but I don't know who the family would be now.

My parents were from the village of Vergate, which was near Milan in northern Italy. My father came over here and his relatives were living up off Stockholm Avenue; there was a road up in there somewhere, and they were living near there. He had his

brother come over and they lived together. My mother and father knew each other over there and then she came over. They had to go to Ellis Island to be married. He went down to meet her and they got married out there. Then they came home here in Pigeon Cove and they had 12 children: 6 boys and 6 girls. Eleven of us survived. One little girl, she was down playing by the pond and fell in and drowned. Right now there's only four of us left, that's all. We're all living to a good old age; I come from an old family. There's Louis ("Gigi") in Pigeon Cove, and Gary Balzarini in Gloucester and a sister, Margaret Fears, in Rockport. Both of my parents were rather small; my mother was really four by four. Attilio ("Niggy") and myself were the two biggest ones in the family.

My father had a farm up on Stockholm Avenue and then moved it down on Curtis Street where the little girl was drowned. He wanted a farm with horses so he sold the house on Curtis Street and we went over to what later was known as the Old Farm Inn but then was called the Babson Farm, bought a pair of horses, went down the farm and that's where we all grew up. The Rockport Granite Company owned the old farm at that time: the quarries were still working and my father wanted to have horses to work in the quarries. So they gave my father the opportunity to rent it. We rented it and all that land that went way down to the shore. We had the pasture on Granite Street. We paid 32 dollars a month! And then it went up to 42 and we thought that was awful. But the Rockport Granite Company was good: we had a silo and they put up a couple of other buildings for my father to use on the farm. I think the farm went from the Babsons to the Olsons, to the Granite Company and then to us.

My mother got tired of working the farm: she milked all the cows. She took care of twelve children and twenty cows. We sold milk around town; we milked twice a day and delivered twice a day at one time, until a new ruling came out that we only had to go out once a day. We always had a big pig pen up in the back. We had the corn fields and the silo: we'd chop up the corn to store it in the fall. The gardens were spectacular: everything you could think of. And my father worked those horses hauling granite for the Granite Company.

As the children came along we all pitched in to take care of them and help raise them. There's nothing like a nice big family. There's always been somebody left. After all these years, there's still four of us left. One by one, we all got married. I got married on the farm and went to an apartment first and then to this place (*235 Granite Street, on the corner of Granite Street and Haven Avenue in Pigeon Cove*). I've been living within a half mile or so of my birthplace all my life.

We've got a picture somewhere of my father on the farm on a winter's day when it was zero out. Charlie Cleaves took a lot of pictures of the farm and I knew him well: him and his daughter Ginny. We didn't have playmates back in those days. We came home from school and helped my mother. We did things like weed and pick the corn, weed the vegetables and flowers. We had no sucha thing as playmates: all we did was sit in school and come right home to my mother; who was a beautiful cook. Oh, could she cook, and she cooked for all of us. We always had very good food. At one time my mother was cooking for seventeen of us: we had

roomers too. But we pitched in and helped and we learned that way.

I still do all my own cooking: I bake and have everything my own. We didn't have time for play. We'd go to church on Sundays. I went to the Lanesville Catholic church at first and when I was confirmed I went over here (*to Rockport*) to Saint Joachims. We used to walk to Lanesville to church. When I was young we didn't have any transportation.

Later on they had a waiting station for the electric cars right out here (*the corner of Haven Avenue and Granite Street*) and right across the street here OddieBoy Woolford's family had an ice cream shop. Oddieboy was a hard one: Charlie Balestraci got in with OddieBoy and he was a hard one too. Sunday afternoons the two of them would go down on Phillips Avenue and race their horses. We'd go down and watch the horse races: that was our outing. I think there was money there somewhere but we didn't pay to watch. The Balestracis came from a more southern part of Italy than the Balzarinis. Charlie had that gas station over in Rockport: he was a good worker but he had a good time too.

Between my father and the Charlie Balzarini on Curtis Street they brought 19 children up between the two of them. We were just like one big family: 'cause they lived only a couple of doors up from us on Curtis Street. We still are like a big family; we always were very close. Mario Balzarini used to do the snow plowing; his nickname was Minkie: I don't know how he got that. And Louie was called Gigi. . .a shortening of Luigi. And my brother Attilio was nicknamed Niggy. He got that because when he was little he used to play with a little black doll and he picked up the name from that.

(No such thing as being politically correct or incorrect back then)

My father left the old Babson Farm and bought what is now Windhover at 257R Granite Street in 1932. My father was a good saver and was able to save enough to buy that place. And he owned all those fields along Phillips Avenue too. . .that whole area was his. He had horses, cows and pigs there and used to go up to Pigeon Hill to make the hay for feed. After my father died my brother Charlie inherited it but it was too big a place for one person so he sold it to the Hahns and took an apartment down the street.

We used to drive the cows up on Pigeon Hill from the Old Farm in the morning; me, my sister and my brother Charlie. We'd drive them up to the top of Pigeon Hill *(a distance of nearly a mile and a half)*. Then at twelve o'clock we'd drive them down to Big Pit* *(at the corner of Rowe Avenue and Drumlin Road)* so they could drink some water. On those hot summer days we'd go swimming with the cows.

Then when the four o'clock whistle blew at the Tool Company we'd drive the cows back home. My mother would make a lunch and my father would bring it to us on Pigeon Hill and we'd eat it while we tended the cows. I still love a farm. I love chickens. We had chickens at the Old Farm: we had everything there, it was a big farm. Now if my brother Charlie had been here he could have told you plenty. Gigi is sixteen years younger than I am. Nobody in my family has lived to be my age yet. Nobody got to be ninety even. But they all made it into their eighties.

We didn't have much time for games but we did manage to go out under a light on the telephone pole at the corner in the evening to play tag or hide and seek. My older sister and I used to take the electric car on Saturday night and go to Gloucester for some shopping. We'd top it off with some ice cream and that was some treat. We did go to the movies once in a while. There was really nothing much else going on around; no money in those days.

I went through the ninth grade in the Rockport schools. The babies were coming and my mother needed help so I had to stay home and help but I was a good student when I was in school. The church was not all that big in our family even though my father knew all the religious holidays but he didn't go to church and my mother didn't either. My mother stayed home and cooked for us when we came home.

Back on the old farm we didn't have central heat, just stoves. We didn't even have a hot water tank. We used to keep the old kettle on the kitchen stove. We had a kitchen stove and we burned wood and coal: it was nice and comfy there. At night my father would come upstairs and put us all to bed. Sometimes my mother and father would go up ahead of us and light those Perfection oil burners to have a little heat in the bedrooms. After we were all in bed my father would take those burners away. Those things were so dangerous. We had three beds in each room, two to a bed, and a corner cot. We always had plenty of bedding. For a bath we used to heat the water on the stove and

*The woods of Pigeon Cove are home to many abandoned granite quarries, now filled with rain and spring water making magnificent swimming holes. Locals call them pits. Many of these once fully employed holes in the ground are now privately owned.

bring a wash tub up to our room and took our baths there. You don't know now what a way that was to live: but we didn't know the difference back then.

I learned to can and preserve fruit and vegetables after I got married. At one time I did a couple of hundred jars every year. I have a little vegetable garden and I still do all my tomatoes.

One thing different nowadays from the old days is that some things are right out in the open. They happened in the old days but they happened behind closed curtains. In the old days we used to go down into the Cove and buy 'most everything. Ferdinand Orne had a meat market there. On the corner of Granite and Breakwater Avenue there was a hardware store. And there was an ice cream parlor in Pigeon Cove: it was a drug store and then they put ice cream with it. Abbie Mason used to run a rooming house on the corner of Mt. Locust and Haven Avenues. They rented rooms and served meals. Mr. Mason ran the drug store. A Mr. Niemi had a cobbler shop in the Cove. And the harbor came right up to the road where the old Tool Company parking lot is today. They had an iron fence to keep people from falling down on the beach there.

I got married in 1928 to Rudolph "Doodle" Anderson and we had three children. He grew up just a few doors up from the Old Farm. We were married 62 years when he died. He only had one job all his working life: die sinker down at the Tool Company, 49 years. They wanted him to stay to get the fifty years in but he wasn't feeling good so he said he couldn't do that and had to give up and was in and out of the hospital. But he was retired for 27 years! He died at 92 years old. My son Russell says he's

counting on this longevity.

I get along good with my neighbors. I like them all and we all get along. But I don't like the style of dropping in for a cup of coffee. In the morning, when I get up, I want to do my chores and be ready just in case someone calls and says lets go and do so and so. I want to be ready. I don't want to postpone my chores by visiting others. I go up the line and do shopping, lunch out, I go out all the time. I do all my house work; my laundry my cleaning, my cooking and baking, everything: I do it all. I just made an apple pie. But I'm getting lazy; I can't do my housework like I used to. I do what I can but I can't do it any more. The boys say it's all right, we'll do it for you and I say, "No, I don't want any boys in my house!" I tell them that I'll do what I can, that's all. My boys are beautiful cooks; both of them. And so is Gigi: I tell them I don't know where they got it, I don't have it.

My brother Gigi worked for Niggy in the construction business all his life and retired when he hit 65. Gigi lost his wife and I lost Rudy within 13 days of each other and my brother Charlie died right after that: in 27 days we lost three of the family. That was a blow. Gigi lives all alone up on Pigeon Hill Street and has a big garden and a lot of fruit trees. He does a lot of cooking. He's always bringing me things he's cooked. When he bakes bread he always brings me a loaf.

In times back we thought that a lot of Rockporters used to look down their noses at Pigeon Covers. Back in the early days, when so many Pigeon Covers, mostly immigrants; Finns, Swedes, Italians, worked in the quarries many of the houses in Pigeon Cove were more like shacks than homes. After the War (World War II) when people began to make more money they began to build them all up, but back then the Cove was thought of as a pretty poor place. All those early Covers had big families. Back then you had a big family in hopes that enough of the kids would make enough to be able to take care of their parents in their old age. Nowadays whatever the parents have left over, it goes to the kids. But a little hardship is good for anybody. Parents today don't teach the kids to take care of things and make do with what they can afford. You can't blame the kids, they don't know the difference. When we grew up my father was very frugal and we learned our lesson. When we grew up we all owned our own home.

I've been across three or four times. Me and my two sisters and sister-in-law went over together. We went to Italy, Switzerland and way down to the end of the Italian boot. The first time we spent two weeks and had such a good time we went back the next year for two more weeks. We went to Spain and Portugal that time. And I've been out on a lot of those senior citizen bus trips in this country: New York, Washington, a lot of places. I stay busy.

Laying the deep water trench up Pigeon Hill on what is now named Landmark Lane, probably during the Great Depression. Work of this kind was mandated to be done by hand to keep people gainfully employed.

ROBERT ANDERSON

Born in Rockport in 1917, on the same property he now lives on at 25 King Street, on the shore of the Mill Pond, just up the street from Front Beach.

MY MOTHER AND FATHER came to this country from Finland in the early 1900's. I grew up with four older sisters. Being the youngest and the only boy in the family I got a lot of privileges and protection. In the winter if I coughed or sneezed more than once they thought I was catching a cold and immediately get a jar of Musterol rub for my chest and Father John's cough medicine. The Musterol was so strong it made my eyes water and the Father John's tasted like it must have been ninety percent castor oil.

When the cold and flu season was in sway my mother would sprinkle powdered sulphur on the hot kitchen stove. It would burn with a blue flame and give off a very peculiar smell. She said it would kill germs and I believed her. A few days before Christmas my mother started to prepare a traditional Scandanavian dish called "lukefisk" which was made from dried salt cod, and was as hard as a stonewall. The salted dried fish was first soaked in a lye solution followed by three or four changes of fresh water, until the lye and salt were removed. Only then was it ready to be cooked.

Our Christmas tree wasn't like those well groomed Christmas trees we see on sale these days. More than likely it was a white pine with long, soft pine needles and had grown up around Third Pines, which was between Evans Field and Briar Swamp. We dragged it through the woods down to King Street and put up in a corner of our living room. Most of our tree decorations were home-made. The girls made long chains from strips of paper, colored with crayons and the ends stuck together with a paste made from flour and water. Then the paper chain was hung on the tree. Electricity hadn't reached our house early on so we bought small metal candle holders and clipped them to the branches. Larger candles were stuck to the windowsills in the living room. How we managed to avoid burning the house down amazes me.

We opened our presents on Christmas morning, most of which were clothing: woolen sweaters, mittens and stockings. Ma got a new apron among her gifts which she proudly wore as she made our lukefisk dinner which had bits of hard-boiled egg in the sauce. Being together, healthy, and having fun was another gift we all shared.

On New Year's Eve our family gathered around the kitchen table and had home-made fudge, popcorn and home-made root beer. We had to pour out the root beer cautiously so the yeast that had settled on the bottom didn't get stirred up. We all liked to have our fortunes told at that time. My mother had a unique way of telling our fortunes. She heated a piece of lead in an iron ladle until it turned to liquid, then quickly poured it into a kettle of ice-cold water. By the time the lead reached the bottom of the kettle it had become solid again but it had been transformed into many strange shapes. My mother told our fortunes by "reading" the shapes which had formed in the kettle.

I have lived near the Mill Pond for 80+ years and know nearly every tree, every rock around or near the pond. I've seen every bird and animal that lives there and caught just about every kind of fish that swam in the pond. Most of my growing up years were spent around the pond and sometimes in it; which always brought a scolding from my mother when I came in the house with wet, muddy shoes. We fed small minnows from the pond to my mother's hens until she complained that the eggs tasted fishy: that took care of that.

In the winter we skated on the pond and played a lot of hockey. Sometimes there were 8 to 10 players on each side. There was no limit, as long as you had a hockey stick or a bent tree branch you played hockey. There was one guy who loved to play but I never saw him with skates on so we let him play goal tender. We called him Ruggles. He took a lot of flying pucks on his shins and one day we suggested that he should get himself a pair of shin guards. He said he already had some. He pulled up his pants and he had Life magazines wrapped around his lower legs. The game went on.

I went through all the Rockport schools, none of which either exist or are used as school buildings any more. I went to the Beach Street school first: the American Legion Hall at present. The George J. Tarr School on School Street, now the Rockport public library. The Broadway School, which was where the Police and Fire Station was built in 1939. And I graduated in 1935 from the Rockport High School at the foot of Broadway, now used as affordable apartments for senior citizens.

We used to swim in the water filled granite quarries. No one wore a bathing suit. We thought nothing of it; everyone looked alike: more or less. One sunny summer afternoon there was a party of surveyors on top of Pigeon Hill with their tripod, glass, plumb bob and stick, trying to figure out who owned what around these swimming holes. Earlier that afternoon a young couple who had been skinny dipping in a nearby quarry were sunning themselves on a nice flat, hot granite ledge. The surveyors picked them up in their scope and there wasn't much land surveying done the rest of that afternoon.

Rockport was a happy and fun place to grow up in in the 1920's and 1930's. We had no television; frozen foods were unheard of, no contact lenses, or frisbees, or Pill. We never knew FM radio, tape decks, vinyl phonograph records, yogurt, artificial hearts, or guys wearing earrings and girls with pierced noses and other things. We never had much when I was growing up but we made the most of what we had. We didn't know credit cards, dishwashers, or electric blankets. There were no pizzas, MacDonalds or instant coffee. We thought fast food was what you ate during Lent. We knew five and dime stores where you could buy things for five and ten cents. For one nickel you could make a phone call, buy a Pepsi or enough stamps to mail one letter and two postcards.

Those were the times when a chip meant a piece of wood and software wasn't even a word. You could buy a Chevy coupe for around $600, but not many could afford one: a pity, because gasoline was eleven cents a gallon. Cigarette smoking was fashionable back then, grass was what we mowed, coke was a drink and pot was something you cooked in. Rock music was a grandma's lullaby and aids were helpers in the principal's office.

Up the Boston & Maine railroad tracks toward the Loop Pond* there was a shallow

---

*Loop Pond: a loop of railroad tracks off the main rails about a half mile back toward Gloucester, which was used to back the steam locomotives around in order for them to be in the front of the train headed back to Boston. It was more a swamp than a pond in the center of the loop.

culvert that ran under the tracks. When we would hear a train coming down the line from Gloucester we crawled into that culvert and were thrilled when the big steam locomotive thundered overhead and filtered sand and gravel down upon us. After the last passenger car went above us toward the depot we crawled out and dusted ourselves off, still excited by the closeness of those rattling wheels.

We liked to walk down Bearskin Neck and go to Howard Hodgkin's wharf, now called Tuna Wharf. Howard had a fish and lobster market. Out near Milk Island he also maintained a fish trap. Just about every morning Howard's trap boat left the harbor and went out to the Milk Island trap. When they came back their dory was full of fish; some still flapping around. Some days the catch would be mackerel and other days cod or "Old England" (*whiting*). The mackeral was a beautiful fish. When the sun rays hit the fish many bright colors were seen but when the fish died the colors faded away.

The artist's ball was held in the old Town Hall in late August and was always a big attraction. We would watch the people entering the Hall in their costumes; some very colorful and original; some very brief. At one of these events a few young ladies became a bit too boisterous and were brought to the local lockup to sober up. In the morning the officer on duty brought them bowls of corn flakes for their breakfast. One of the ladies began yelling in a loud voice, "I want some Kotex! I need some Kotex!" The officer responded by telling her that Kotex be damned, she'd get corn flakes just like all the others.

At one time they showed moving pictures in the old Town Hall* on Saturday nights. The doors opened at seven o'clock and Everett Sanborn was always the first one there. He'd have a white knuckle grip on the doorknob and when the doors were opened he'd take those stairs up to the balcony in the auditorium three at a time to get his favorite seat in the front row. Everett would entertain us while we waited for the movie to start. Police officer "Doggie" Blatchford would patrol the hall and maintain order. When we became too noisy Doggie would look up to the balcony and stare hard at us and we'd quiet right down. We knew that if we didn't he'd have us out on the sidewalk in a minute.

The early movies then were silent movies: no sound tracks. We had an excellent lady piano player who played along with the pictures. When the movie became exciting she'd really pound those keys, and if the pictures were sad or dramatic she'd play quietly and mournfully enough to make you cry: the movie and the piano became as one. Movies back then didn't have all the blood and guts that we see in pictures and TV shows today. We didn't need them then and we don't really need them now.

In August, 1936 I joined the C.C.C

---

*The old Town Hall was on the site of the present Town Hall. It was a stately old three story wooden structure which had town offices and some stores at one time on the ground floor. On the second floor was a large auditorium containing a basketball court, a stage with a proscenium arch and a balcony: over 500 people could be comfortably seated on this floor. On the third floor were meeting halls which housed, among other groups, a Masonic Lodge. It was thought the building had outlived its usefulness and a committee decided that it made sense to tear it down and a town meeting so voted it. Much to everyone's dismay and disgust, it was still so sound that it took many more weeks to tear it down than had been predicted and the town has not had such a wonderful meeting place since. A far cry from today's cracker box.

(*Civilian Conservation Corps: a Federal work program to put people to work in the Great Depression*) and was at a camp located on Savoy Mountain out near North Adams. We built roads through the State Park in the summer. In the winter we cut and thinned out hard wood trees from the evergreen forest. The camp hired on a few older men who lived in the area and knew the woods and trails we worked in. We called them "Apple Knockers." One of these guys asked if he could borrow my suitcase over the weekend. I lent it to him and never saw him again. Our wooden, tar paper covered barracks had wood-burning stoves for heat and we took turns keeping them going during the bitter cold winter nights. The wind blew most of the time and it snowed a lot. The following spring I left the C.C.C.

I worked for a while for Eric Pearson, as his mason tender. He lived on Hale Street. When I worked for him his main work was topping off chimneys on some of the two and a half story mansions in Magnolia. I had to bring bricks and mortar to him up on the roof over a tall ladder. By the time I got back to the bottom of the ladder he was out of bricks and mortar already. The plaster he used on interior walls of houses was made of lime, cement and horse hair, mixed with a hoe. I got paid $20 a week.

Right around the corner from here was (*and still is*) Forest Street, better known in those days as Finn Alley because of the many Finnish families living there. They were honest, hard working people. Most of the men worked in the granite quarries. They left early in the morning with their lunch pails, walking up through Manning Park (*across Granite Street from the upper end of Forest Street*) to the quarries. There were two Finn stores on Forest Street: one belonged to Jack Walima and the other to Emil Ranta. They both sold fresh produce, great Finn rye bread and coffee ground right from the beans. In the "cold room" fresh beef was cut from a side of beef and ground into hamburg right before our eyes. We also bought kerosene for our two burner Perfection kitchen stoves from them. The round burners had isinglass windows in them so you could see the wicks and how much flame you had. You could telephone your order in and they would write it down and add it up with lead pencils on paper order blanks and then deliver it to your house.

During the Great Depression years (*1929 to 1939*) many families had to do without many necessary items. Some couldn't afford to have their shoes repaired or resoled so when the soles wore through they put cardboard over the holes. Some stores began to sell what we used to call "Depression soles". These were thin pieces of rubber with glue on one side. If we put them on properly they would stay and last a long time. Sometimes they would loosen up and would flap when you walked and then everyone knew you were wearing depression soles. Parents did the best they could.

In the early 1940's I worked for the Cape Ann Tool Company* in Pigeon Cove. After I was hired they told me to buy a pair of safety shoes and report for work the next day. I walked across Granite Street from the Tool Company office to Andrew Niemi's shoe store and he said that if I didn't have the money for the shoes I could come back on payday with it. He was a great person and

---

*The Tool Company was closed some years ago and has been the source of a continuing controversy about how that site might be developed. At this writing it is still unresolved.

always a gentleman.

I worked in the forge shop, grinding stock and also at the cold presses. I also worked with Albert Wilson who lived on Squam Hill and ran the 2500 pound steam hammer. Sometimes nuts and bolts would fly off the hammer and rattle off the wall behind us: hard hat country. But hard hats weren't heard of back then, neither were ear protectors. After a man had worked for months or years at one of those hammers, banging out forgings, his hearing would not be so great. They used to say that hammer men had "drop hammer ears."

The Tool Company was working around the clock on war work at that time and I worked the 8pm to 6am shift. Working in front of those furnaces heating the blocks of steel we wore long underwear winter and summer for protection from the heat. In the summer the big doors on the street side of the building were kept open and passersby could look in and watch the hammers bang the white hot bars of steel into forgings. They had a barrel on a cart that came around and the barrel was filled with water, salt, oatmeal and a block of ice. I guess the salt was to replace what we lost from perspiring and the oatmeal was for added nourishment. Whatever it was, the drink tasted terrific because it was cold.

In October of 1942 I joined the Navy and was put on an aircraft carrier which joined the 3rd Fleet in the Pacific. My battle station was at a twin 40mm antiaircraft cannon. One of my other duties was as an orderly (aide) to the executive officer, who was second in command of the carrier. When he wasn't roaming around the ship I was stationed outside his office door and took messages to him when they came into the radio shack, and I always took a quick glance at

them first. When I returned to my living quarters my shipmates would always ask me what the latest "scoop" was. In my division we had an American Indian from Oklahoma. We never called him by his given name: we called him Chief. But he didn't care because he was very proud of his heritage.

On November 20, 1943, off the coast of Tarawa, our ship was hit by a torpedo from a Japanese airplane but a good damage control crew helped keep the vessel afloat. On New Year's Day, 1944, we sailed under the Golden Gate Bridge into dry dock at Hunters Point. We got patched up there and converted into the Navy's first night operating carrier and went back out under the bridge once more to join Admiral "Bull" Halsey's Pacific fleet. One of our sailors took a shine to a woman welder working on repairing the ship. They dated and later married. They are celebrating their 50th wedding anniversary on July 20, 1999.

Off the Phillipines our task force got hit by a violent typhoon. The wind was fierce and the waves were like small mountains, with visibility about zero. Many of our planes were damaged and three destroyers; the Spence, the Monahan and the Hull rolled over and sank. The crews didn't have a chance because most of them were below decks on account of the weather. Very few survived.

We stood off Okinawa for about three months, being supplied by tankers and freighters, and every day the Jap kamkazies came over. A Jap plane dropped a bomb on the carrier Franklin about a quarter mile away from us. The bomb went through the flight deck and exploded down below; quickly starting fires on the hanger deck where some planes were parked, armed and gassed up. They started to burn and blow up and a gas line ruptured so that burning aviation fuel poured over the side of the ship like a firey waterfall. A cruiser came alongside the stricken carrier to try to put out the fires and some cruiser crewmen were killed by falling debris. The rest of our ships had to keep moving and soon the Franklin was only a column of black smoke on the horizon.*

After the Phillipine's liberation and the Okinawa campaign the war soon ended. While we were anchored in Tokyo Bay I became eligible for discharge from the service and got back home in early October, 1945.

Back once again in Rockport after three years I found the town hadn't changed all that much except a lot of guys I knew weren't around any more. I worked a while for a local mason contractor but this was only a seasonal job. So I got a job with the Town Department of Public Works, working to put down new water mains and driving a snow plow. I finished up my work for the Town by helping to operate the water filtration plant on Upper Main Street. I later worked for Gloucester Engineering in Gloucester and the Home Center in Essex, and sold lobsters with my lobsterman son Mike at Haymarket Square in Boston.

Today I still live on the same property, near the Mill Pond, where four generations of Andersons have lived. I stay at home pretty much these days. I enjoy being able to watch the young kids play around the pond; fishing in it and ice skating on it. What goes around comes around.

---

*In one of the most daring and unusual feats of seamanship during the Pacific war with Japan the Franklin was saved. I've seen pictures of her, listing so heavily as to be improbable, aflame from nearly stem to stern with the burning gasoline Bob mentions as it poured into the sea from the bowels of the vessel. My cousin Jay Oker was a crew member aboard the Franklin at that time and says he was just plain lucky to have survived the inferno. He was down below when the Franklin was struck and his area immediately filled with thick black smoke so dense he couldn't see anything. He flapped his arms about trying to find something to grab and was fortunate to bump into a ladder which took him topside. There he witnessed the Catholic chaplain administering last rites all over the deck that wasn't in flames. That priest later got the Distinguished Service Cross for his actions that terrible day. The Franklin was eventually saved and limped all the way back to the Brooklyn Navy Yard where she put in for repairs. She never again saw active service.

Cows pastured atop Pigeon Hill, probably before water tower and homes. Smoke belches from the Cape Ann Tool Company chimney down below with Andrews Point in far distance.

MYRON BROWN

Born in Rockport in 1915. Most of Myron's working life was spent in the U. S. Postal Service, like his father before him. Myron wound up his career as Rockport Postmaster for five years or so. But he has had a lifelong inter-est in sailing and as a young sailor was present at the very beginning of the present Sandy Bay Yacht Club on the end of T Wharf. Some of Myron's fondest memories are centered on the Yacht Club.

"My father and others in the family were all interested in town genealogy and I grew up with that kind of thing: who is related to who and so forth. A lot of stuff happened fifteen or twenty years before I was born but I remember it from hearing so much about it.

MY GRANDMOTHER Wilson's maiden name was Silva. The Silvas lived on a farm: Cutty Jeppson's house on Broadway Terrace, right in back of where Broadway Avenue is today. My mother grew up there. There was no Broadway in those days. Parker Street and High Street were in place but no Broadway as we know it. It was all farm land around there then. And of course, George Todd had cows on Parker Street. *(The cow barns are still standing behind 8 Parker Street).*

My grandfather Sears came from Portugal.* He came from the old country but my grandmother Silva was born in this country. He was a fisherman. The Portuguese came as crews for fishing boats; they were mostly whalers. When the whalers would stop at the Azores and were short handed they'd pick up some Azorean Portuguese whalers and then two or three

years later they'd eventually land in Gloucester and Rockport. The Portuguese fishermen were deep sea men while the Gloucester Italian fishermen were inshore fishermen. The Portuguese were used to fish-ing off the Grand Banks from their home ports and the Italian fishermen fished much closer to shore: a different kind of fishing altogether.

At one time there was a large number of Newfie (*Newfoundlanders*) fishermen on the Cape, having come here much the same way as the Portuguese: when local vessels pulled into ports in Newfoundland and Nova Scotia and needed extra crewmen or cabin boys and the like, they'd pick them up in the Canadian Maritimes and they would even-tually land on the Cape also. The Browns came to Rockport from Maine. Like so many others, they came as fishermen.

I was born at 22 High Street. My grand-mother was midwife at my birthing. When I was about 10 years old my father moved us up to 32 High Street: I grew up there, went through high school. Once I got married I bought a house at 28 High Street, where my children were born. I still own that house. My daughter and my son live there.

My playmates included the Greens down on lower High Street, Babe, Bob and Earl Green, Merrill McLane, Tony Pascucci. Tony was my buddy all the way through school, the whole young Pascucci family, and then in the Boy Scouts I got to know about all the kids in town. Laddie Reddy, Johnny Lamb, Austin Cushman, the Hanson family are some that come to mind.

I played most sports when I was growing

*Bill Francis says all Cape Ann Sears were Soares in the original Portuguese.

up. 'Course I knew all the kids in the Boy Scouts during that time; my father was Scout Master. We used to have Scout cabins in the Southern woods: they were built and maintained by guys like Russell Lachman and George Parker, and the Seligs up on Great Hill. We used to spend our winters roaming around the woods and our summers at the beach. In the springtime the bugs always drove us out of the woods so we ended up on the seashore.

We used to march in the Memorial Day parades in the Scouts. In those early days we still had old members of the GAR* living in town and they always thought Memorial Day was their day. But after World War I those veterans wanted to participate and the GAR guys weren't too happy about that. So they split the day in half: the morning was the American Legion parade and speeches and the afternoon was the GAR vets day. The Scouts marched in both parades and had a nice meal after each parade so they made out very well. Then after the last parade there would be a band concert in the Town Hall yard. After dark we all went upstairs in the Town Hall and watched a movie.

When I got a bit older than the Boy Scout days I got to hanging around at the "University of Star Island"**: Herb Rich's gang. Herb was wonderful with us kids. Myself, Duffy Blatchford, Spencer Perkins and a lot of other kids throughout the town, we were all graduates of Star Island. We used to hang out there and it was a two-way

thing. He got a lot of work out of us , but in the doing of it he taught us how to tie rope, knit lobster heads for lobster pots, how to go fishing. Herb always had his skiff tied up there and we learned how to tie the knot he tied it up with. Then you could use it, but only so long as you tied it back up properly. He used to go lobstering and took out fishing parties and one or two of us kids would tag along to bait the hooks and generally help out. He also had an old Friendship sloop that he revived and put new sails on and he took sailing parties out on her. We learned our first things about sailing from Herb Rich's Friendship sloop. The one still remaining building on Star Island was refurbished by Peter Tuttle years ago; that was Herb's fish house. Dick Rich and Chester Gott had fish houses there also. Chester was just the opposite of Herb Rich: he didn't want much to do with us kids. Chester was a ship's carpenter who went lobstering; he lived over on Gott Street. He was Betty Wilson Engel's grandfather.

When I hung out on Star Island, T Wharf had no yacht club. There was the Todd coal "pocket" and the burned out remains of the old fish freezer on the end. The end was just an empty dock. When they started to build the yacht club I was right there watching them. Gus deGalt was an old fisherman who lived by himself and he had a yacht that had caught afire once and he rebuilt it enough so it'd float. Old Gus lived on the boat; it was tied up at the end of the wharf, where the floats are now. He did some

---

*The GAR stood for the Grand Army of the Republic, Union veterans from the U. S. Civil War. The present Christian Science Church on Main Street was originally the GAR Hall and the plaque can still be seen on the front of that building.

**Star Island was not an island, but a rock strewn stretch of coastline off Atlantic Avenue, across the cove from the end of T Wharf .

fishing and was an old bachelor who lived there by himself.

Now back in 1885 there was what some have called the original Sandy Bay yacht club which consisted of a dozen or so wealthy people who had boats. . .this was about the time the Hunter Harwoods came to town. This small group used the last building on Bearskin Neck as their headquarters.

But the present yacht club really began when the town held a celebration: I don't exactly what it was for but it was a community wide celebration. One of the features of this celebration was an invitation to yachts from all the local yacht clubs; Eastern Point, Annisquam, Marblehead, to come to our harbor. At that time there were not many pleasure sailboats in Rockport harbor. It was primarily a working harbor, lobster and fishing boats. Some of us kids had a few small sailboats but no real yachts here. So they had this big regatta and the whole town got excited about sailing, the entire town was really excited about sailing.

My brother Dyke and I had a small sailboat when we were in high school and we used to sail it around. We liked to sail. We knew something about it with our Star Island experiences. Our sailing really began back in the Boy Scouts when we found an old sloop on the beach in the inner harbor behind Gene Thibeault's market (*the present Greenery Restaurant.*) We tracked down the owner (it was somebody over in Pigeon Cove) and he donated it to us. We patched it together and Marion Cooney* furnished

sails for it. We called it the Boy Scout boat and sailed it around, a thirty four (or 24) footer. We had a lot of fun there.

So after this regatta stirred up a new interest in sailing, Marion Cooney called a meeting of interested boat owners and it was held in the old Granite Savings Bank. They wound up with a group of fifty persons: all local people, all year 'rounders. Louie Rogers and Lindley Dean and people like that, people with money, carried it while it got started. These fifty people backed the club and they decided to build their club on the end of T Wharf. Marion Cooney struck a contract with Everett Wilkinson, a local who was a contractor up in Boston, to build the club for $5000. All this came about in 1930. From then on practically everything else that was done at the club was done by volunteer help. In those Depression days people weren't working anyway so it didn't cost them anything to give a day's work to the club. The first club derrick was a wooden one from the Leonard Johnson quarry, one that was used to hoist the granite out of the quarry. The necessary iron work was done by the Cape Ann Tool Company. We spent one winter building the wooden pontoons for use as floats in the summer.

T Wharf was town property but nobody thought anything of it: the club was a town project and there was no protest. They wound up there for over 20 years before the town decided they should be paying some kind of rent. It was the people in town who started it and saw that it got built. People like Pete Perkins and 'Fonse (or Con)

---

*Marion Cooney ran a sail loft in Gloucester and supplied sails for the Gloucester fishing schooners as well as sailing yachts. When the schooners day was done he made canvas covers and awnings for naval vessels, his big account was the Bath Iron Works in Maine. He also made canvas sea and duffle bags for the various military services in World War II.

Thibeault bought a boat together, one of those old Fish boats, probably paid $300 for it and they sailed it. It was quite a fleet. The Coast Guard was a big help: they patrolled the races and towed us in after dark if we got becalmed.

Now that they had a club they needed boats to sail with. So they went to John Alden, the Boston boat designer, and asked for a design for Sandy Bay. Keep in mind that this was at the height of the Depression. They had the Graves boatyard in Marblehead build these boats, just to keep the crew busy during this bad time. Gifford Beal, Lindley Dean, Chester Story, and Johnny Chiancola, a fish dealer from Gloucester signed up to buy one. They cost something like $1600, big money in the Depression. These were keeled 24 footers.

In the meantime, while the Sandy Bays were being built, the Nahant Dory Club had a fleet of Star boats and they were sort of disbanding. They were selling off the Star boats at rake-off prices. Marian Cooney took his power boat to Nahant and towed the Stars bought by Rockporters to the harbor. The new owners were Pierce Grover, Frank Grover, Ralph Hale, Guy Hale and Max Kuehne. So the club had five Star boats to start sailing with. Before this we had races of any kind of boat against any other kind of boat; we had no classes of boats early on. Charlie Pierce had an Annisquam Bird boat and Dyke and I had this little 23 footer, Gifford Beal had a 17 foot open sailboat, Max Kuehne had a Fish boat, and Ben Knutsen had a canoe-like boat with an outrigger to it that he sailed. But the Star boats were and still are the class of racing sailboats. They are two man, 23 footers and are considered the yachtsmen violins: tuned to the nth degree. All your big time sailors,

Dennis Connor and others, they all started out in Star boats. Most of the improvements in sailing come from what has been learned in Star boats.

The very first class boats in Rockport harbor were the Pilot boats. Originally there was Hosea Tufts, Marian Cooney and Lindley Dean who had Pilot boats. They were built by the Graves Marblehead boatyard as a step up from the Brutal Beast class of boats. Elliot Grimes owned the last Pilot boat in the harbor.

With the introduction of class boats we became a real yacht club but Marion Cooney's idea of the Rockport Yacht Club was that it was a local club composed of local people who liked to sail and should stay local. He used to emphasize that we shouldn't allow it to become Eastern Point or Corinthian or any other fancy club. . .to stick with small town sailing. For a long time he kept the officers of the club local. . .no out of towners need apply for any top position. The summer people came in right away but they were only here three months of the year. They were typified by Joe Lockett down on Old Garden Road, next to Paul Woodbury's place. The McGillians summered and sailed here. The artistic community was represented by the Beal brothers, Gifford and Reynolds, Galen Perrett and Max Kuehne.

During the winter months we used to have a regular Saturday night supper. Each family would put on a Saturday night supper. This, of course, was strictly local people, the summer people having gone back to their winter quarters. There was no running water in the club in the winter: we carried water for coffee down from Toby Leaman's First National (*on the right side of the head of T Wharf*) in a big wash tub. This was some coffee: they used cheesecloth to hold the coffee in the tub and boiled it over the stove; they had a good galley there. They got so popular for a while that we didn't have room enough for all the people who wanted to attend. We used to have near 100 people at these Saturday night suppers.

And during the winter months it became a hangout for members: sort of a substitute for the Social Club up over the old National Bank on Main Street. The most of them ended up down at the yacht club. Almost any night would find a group there playing cribbage or whist and shooting the breeze. As a kid I used to hang out there a lot: if I only had had a tape recorder back then to get down some of those fellas; the stories they used to tell.

When they started the club up, Marion Cooney was elected commodore and Lindley Dean was vice commodore. Frank Pierce was a character. I can see him now, standing on the end of T Wharf with a wrecking bar in his hand, determined to keep the Italian fishing boats from mooring to the wharf. David McD Martin was the first club steward. He was an Englishman who came over here to work at the Cable Company and always signed his name McD Martin, which some of us thought was presumptuous of him. He lived on Norwood Avenue and was Ford Martin's father. My brother Alvin was steward for a couple of years: he used to sail with Doc Wheeler.

When a lot of these people came into the club with boats they needed some help because most of them didn't know how to sail. They needed a crew. Dyke and I, Duffy Blatchford, Musty Somers, Leo DeCoste: fellas like these put their sailing experience to work teaching the newcomers how to sail. A lot of the original members served as com-

modore for a few years at a crack. Galen Perrett had a power boat when he joined the club and he eventually donated the boat to the club for use as a committee boat.

Class sailboat racing really came into its own in the middle to late 30's. 'Most anybody with a sailboat was in Marblehead during their race week: it was the thing to do. Quite a gang from here used to go down there. One time Marion Cooney bought an old boat; pretty good size, a big yacht actually, probably a sixty footer, no engine in it. Marion always bought cheap and sold for a profit and I think this was one of those purchases. He had the boat anchored in the North Basin. Come Marblehead week he had the Coast Guard tow that boat up to Marblehead and he anchored it in Marblehead harbor. We went up there and stayed on her for the week.

Paul Woodbury came here right after the war. He had grown up in Annisquam sailing Star boats and he was a real good sailor. Paul was good at anything, he was an MIT man: he could do 'most anything. He did things a different way; I spent a lot of time sailing with Paul and he'd come up with some original things: he'd find different ways to do things. I sailed with Paul as far away as Long Island and Newport. We'd trailer his Star boat over the roads. Being with the Post Office I had sick and leave time so I could do that and not lose a day's pay. He had a sail loft above his garage on Old Garden Road.

Marion Cooney took me along on some of these sailing races in other places. One time we were in Newport and stayed aboard a boat owned by Cliff Mallory: the head of the Mallory Steamship Company. One of these times we got to know a George Roosevelt: a cousin of Franklin. George was kind of an oddball, he said he was a man with a black mistress and a white maid. He had a big black schooner which he named Mistress and a white tender was named Maid.

After the war started (World War II) the Coast Guard had over 150 men stationed on the Cape, patrolling the shoreline. I was in the Post Office at that time but joined what they called the Coast Guard Reserve; kind of a naval National Guard. I'd go home from the Post Office and go down and fill in where needed at the Straitsmouth Coast Guard station. When we went on patrol we were issued old World War I Springfield rifles with fixed bayonets. One time we saw lights off Andrews Point and we went out in the double ender with fixed bayonets and all but couldn't find anything.

After it looked like the Uboats were no longer a menace they put us on active duty. (*During World War II the Coast Guard functioned as a part of the U. S. Navy*) My draft number had come up and they offered me an exemption because of my government work at the Post Office. But I didn't want to take that way out so I went in. I was married with two kids but there was no question in my mind, it was the thing I had to do.

We were four boys at one time but one brother died when he was three years old. But my other two brothers, Alvin and Carlton "Dyke" are still alive. Alvin was Town Treasurer for years and also Town Meeting Moderator for many years. Dyke was Town Tree Warden for years. And a lot of people remember my father Alvin Sr., who was Boy Scout leader for many generations of Rockporters and worked in the Post Office before me.

My father was involved in town affairs all his life but he never had a paycheck from

the town. It was one of those things; he had a Civil Service job in the Post Office and in a Civil Service job you were not allowed to work in or for any other branch of government. But my father didn't do any of it for pay; he did it because he was interested. As a kid growing up he got involved in town affairs and when I grew up I was known as "Allie" Brown's kid and that opened all the doors in town. I was thinking a while ago that I don't ever remember hearing him say that he was wrong; I don't think he could say it: that whole generation couldn't say it.

My father's real uncle "Uncle Bill" Parsons as he was once known on the New England theatrical circuit, became Rockport Postmaster. In those days you became Postmaster depending upon your political party and whether or not that party was in power in Washington. My father went to work for Uncle Bill as an assistant, doing the book work. Parsons knew from zilch as far as running the Post Office was concerned and my father was a competent young man just out of high school and knew how to keep books. Now this was before Civil Service: Uncle Bill paid my father to help run the business end of things.

My father might well have eventually become Postmaster but at that time you got to be Postmaster by being in one political party or the other, as I say, and when it went out of power you were out of a job. So he opted to stay as assistant Postmaster and had a steady job. When Roosevelt came in a man named Bob Lowe was out because he was a Republican. Bill Powers then became Postmaster. I always claimed that in the town of Rockport the only people who were Democrats were people who were disagreeable, who wouldn't agree with anyone. There was only about a dozen of them and

Powers was the leading one.

I went to work regularly in the Post Office after graduating from Rockport high school. I used to deliver Special Delivery mail while I was still in school so I had some idea of how the place worked. I worked there for 40 years. I wound up as Postmaster for four or five years but by that time the political Postmaster appointments were a thing of the past: the Postmaster General was eliminated from the Federal Cabinet. It was then up to the Civil Service Commission to make such appointments. After Maurice Foley retired as Postmaster I took a Civil Service exam and was appointed from that. I retired in 1975.

I stopped sailing about 10 years ago. The last time I raced was in a Star boat and I pulled my back out. I just about crawled home and spent two days in bed and decided that from then on I'd better stay away from racing. I bought a 24 foot cruising boat and have cruised down along the Maine coast with her. At one time I thought I might find a nice little cottage along on the Maine coast somewhere. The only thing the Maine coast has that we don't have is that they have more of it.

I can't imagine living anywhere else but Rockport. I've got to have the seashore and the woods. Anywhere else I'd start yelling, "Let me outa here!" I wouldn't be able to stand it. We used to go up country, Vermont, New Hampshire, for two or three days to see the foliage and stuff and after that time I just had to see the ocean. When I drove back home I'd go right down to the end of T Wharf just to make sure it was still there.

I can't find anyone to talk to these days. Nobody wants to listen to tales of the old days; they are just not interested. That's why I like to talk to you like this. I had a period of time after I retired when I'd go down to T Wharf and there'd be four or five fellas there who I could talk to for an hour or so, sharing common experiences. But they've all gone now.

The original Motif #1 with two fishing sloops moored on the end of the wharf and lobster boats alongside. Either boat similar to the Nellie Florence on which my grandfather and greatgrandfather went to sea.

EAMES "DOC" CLEAVES

Born in Rockport in 1915 and lived in town all his life. Doc married another native Rockporter, Mary Somers, in 1935 and had four children. They are still together and very much in love.

MY NAME EAMES was once a last name. Ezra Eames was my great, great grandfather. Ezra was very successful in the first Rockport granite quarrying business: made quite a bit of money.* My father's mother was Emma Eames, one of Ezra's five daughters and two sons. I'm a Junior so my father was also named after Ezra. He left $40,000 to each one of his kids besides the house and other assets. That was a lot of money back then. That money all disappeared before I came around.

Ezra came to town when he was quite young and went into the quarry business. He must have been smarter than hell; at one time he owned practically the whole top of Pigeon Hill. He also owned a lot of land around what they used to call the Sheep Pasture, now called Pigeon Hill street. A lot of Swedish people came to live on all that land he owned at one time.

Ezra Eames built that house at 96 Granite Street now owned by the Yankee Clipper Inn. My father was born in that house. While he was being born in one room, his grandfather, old Ezra, died in another room of the same house.

My grandfather, Charlie Cleaves, built the house on Pasture Road where the Garlicks now live. At the foot of Pasture Road on Granite Street are two stone pillars with a C carved into them. My father (*later the well-known Doctor Cleaves who practised in the large white house dominant at Five Corners*) grew up in that house on Pasture Road. Where Ann Fisk now lives was the barn that went with the house: they had cows and horses. My father graduated from MIT, he didn't intend to be a doctor. After he graduated from MIT he didn't know what to do so he went to Harvard Medical school. He was also a good architect from his MIT studies.

I grew up on Main Street, across from Pete Curtis's Newspaper store (*the large house atop an embankment across from the present Nicholas art gallery*). The house next door, where Clara Cleaves had an insurance company, was where Eliza Caldwell lived. She was a schoolteacher in town for over 50 years. She was awful nice to me and my mother. Nellie and Paul Gibbs lived in there after that for a while.

In 1929 my father moved us up to 90 Main Street at Five Corners. I remember when Tom Wilson started the tonic business (Twin Lights) over there on Broadway. His son-in-law Joe Sears, did all the work, and George wound up with it. George's son Pierce runs it now but he can't hardly get any bottles any more, I guess they just don't make 'em any more.

Old Fred Nickerson had that store just off Five Corners on Railroad Avenue (*barely standing today, the first place on the right on Railroad Avenue out of Five Corners*) and

---

*According to Marshall Swan in his book "Town on Sandy Bay" Ezra Eames bought up ledges of granite along Granite Street just before Rockport separated from Gloucester. In 1839 Eames picked up David Babson's interest in the "top field" on Pigeon Hill and in 1840 he built the classic Greek Revival house at 96 Granite Street at the relatively early age of 39: the house he died in and the house where Doc's father was born.

some of his cronies like Gardner Green and Benny Burns used to gather in the back room to smoke and gab and probably take a drink or two. Fred used to keep a bottle down cellar (*in the large house next door to the former store that fronts on Main Street*) behind the furnace. His wife would come down and take his Goddamn bottle and break it. So he went right at her and told her, "Listen, I'll spend every damned cent I've got in the bank and everything you've got in the bank but I'm goin' to have a bottle behind that furnace." And by God he did, right up until he died. I think he had quite a bit of money but he didn't make it in that little store: family must have had it. His father had a grain mill up where the J. Raymond Smith lumber company used to be on Railroad Avenue.

I remember when Loring Grimes owned Bearskin Neck. I don't know where his money came from, I just barely remember him but I think he owned fishing boats. Grimes lived on the corner of Main, Jewett and Cleaves Streets, that big place that's called the Hull House now. Grimes's daughter married Hunter Harwood, the head engineer for the Sandy Bay breakwater (*the outer breakwater near Salvages*). They both died there.

Some of my childhood pals were Herman "Jake" Nelson, "Tinny" Worthley, Sam Henderson, Eddie Orr, and Rudy "Kitty" Oker (*the author's uncle*) . Jake lived up over Joe Pascucci's shoe repair shop (*presently Walter Julian's barbershop, Walter being Joe's son-in-law*) in a building owned by a Doctor Tupper; Tupper's own home was next to the Congregational Church fronting on Main Street. Joe bought the shoe shop building from Dr. Tupper.

Speaking of Walter Julian being the only barber in town: once we had a lot of barbers in Rockport, "Polo" Cooney and his son Harold, Harvey Jodrey, John Francis over in the Cove, Louie Thomas, and Ralph Tarr. Bert Deveau had a barber shop at the foot of Cove Hill that Ralph Tarr eventually took over. Bert used blanc mange (*a seaweed based substance used for many purposes*) for shaving his customers with. He used to say that it not only made for a good shave, it beautified the face. "Skip" Webster was a barber there after Deveau and when Ben Hull was a kid he got a haircut from him. Ben's mother didn't like it and went to him and complained. Skip said, "Now Mrs. Hull, I can't put a two dollar haircut on a ten cent head." Ralph Tarr's wife was a Finnish girl and she always wanted to go back to Finland. She pestered Ralph for years until he finally said OK, we'll go. He bought two tickets and they went to Boston to catch the boat to cross the ocean. Just before they cast off Ralph told his wife to go up ahead on the boat and that he'd be up in a couple of minutes. Ralph turned around and came back to Rockport and she went off to Finland by herself.

I went to Polo Cooney's barber shop for years but went down to Ralph Tarr's shop and played chess there: he always had a chess board set up next to a pot bellied stove. I liked to play chess. I finally decided I couldn't go and play chess without having my hair cut there so I began to have Ralph cut my hair. When Ralph died I started going to Walter Julian: he's been there for 43 years.

I went all through school in Rockport and graduated from high school in 1931. Some of my classmates were Shirley Swanson, later Mrs. Herm Erwin, Tinny Worthley, Jack Reed over in the Cove, Bill Ranta, "Tucker" Hillier. After high school I went to Dean Academy in Franklin, Mass. and graduated from there. It was a beautiful school. I was into sports then: baseball and football. My parents were probably thinking of some career beyond Dean but I wasn't. I didn't get kicked out of Dean but I raised hell for the year I was there. I was slated to go to William and Mary college down in Virginia but I got screwed up somehow. That summer I never went there: I had sent my marks down and was all set to go: too bad I didn't now.

I came back from Dean and worked around some. I worked a bit for the old isinglass factory on Railroad Avenue (the present Isinglass Place). Sam Henderson worked there before me; I think I took Sam's job. They only worked there in the winter: for the cold water used in the machines. There used to be a storage pond next to the building. They used isinglass to settle beer with.* They'd put it in the brew and it would sink slowly to the bottom and take all the sediment with it.

When the isinglass business first started here they used local fish sounds for their product. I guess each fish has a sound: probably part of their "breathing" apparatus. They wound up importing them from India. My job as basket boy was to put the sounds in a basket on the first floor, put that on a dumb waiter kind of rig to the second floor where about 20 women worked: Eben Green's wife, Tinny Worthley's mother, the Lundeen sisters, a whole gang of 'em. I used to know 'em all.

They used to have a ninth grade in Rockport once but they did away with it. The class of '29 was a combination of the eighth grade and the freshman year: they had about 85 in it: Snap Silva, Sam Henderson, Tink Hale, Eddie White, all big strapping guys. They had a good football team back then. Eddie White was in the Marines for quite a while. He came back from the war and built all those houses across from Back Beach: White Way. He used to live up on Hooper Court off Parker Street. His mother kept pigs up there and used to hang 'em up and cut their throats and the women would collect the blood and make blood pudding out of it. The Grays used to live on Hooper Court and kept cows up there at one time.

Ray Rowe started work on the old Boston and Maine Railroad** as a fireman. Ray eventually made it to be an engineer on the Boston to Rockport run. Ray had two brothers, Ebsie and Frazee and all three drank a bit. Frazee's son, Kenny, had all those horses up there near the high school. I worked a year up at the cemetery and Frazee dug all the graves. He was a hard worker, they all were hard workers.

In those days the last couple of trains down from Boston would stay in the roundhouse overnight. The roundhouse wasn't really round but was up the tracks a ways from the depot on the right hand side of the tracks. They'd keep the fires in those locomotives burning all night and in the morning they'd rake the coals, put some more in

---

*A combination of Prohibition and the discovery of chemicals that would do the same thing to beer, spelled the doom of Rockport's isinglass industry. The factory on Railroad Avenue was the last isinglass plant in North America.

**At one time the Boston and Maine was one of Rockport's main employers. Many local residents worked the trains, from the engine to baggage clerks, conductors and ticket agents.

and fire them up, ready to go back to Boston. Spencer Perkins maintained them.

One Sunday a gang was sitting around in Dock Square, Tate Knowlton, Ebsie, Poke Slavin, Polla Hendrickson and Ray and some others and they were awful dry and complaining about it. Finally Ray announced that he'd get them something. Ray walked up to the roundhouse, took one of those engines out and backed it to Gloucester. He went along the tracks as far as Maplewood Avenue in Gloucester, went into a package store to buy a half dozen bottles of booze and took the engine back to Rockport. I don't know how many times Ray did this but he eventually got caught and they fired him. That was a good job, engineer on the trains; he wound up doing house painting. He never talked much but when he drank he'd be uglier than hell.

Speaking of Tate Knowlton, his uncle, Tate Allen who lived down South End was the guy who swam ashore and saved Captain Pitty. They were on one of those Granite Company boats coming back from Boston and the damn thing sank. Captain Pitty couldn't swim and Tate Allen swam ashore in Rockport with Pitty on his back.

There were some old sailing granite carrying vessels moored in Rockport harbor when I was a kid. A big schooner on T Wharf and the Mary A. White over on the Waddell brothers side of the inner harbor. Rodney Pitty, a grandson of Captain Pitty, had a hut down on her, a nice place where the cabin was.

Up by the Haskins hospital on top of Poole's Hill (*Summit Avenue*) was Third Pines. As you went into the hospital grounds there was a road that went off to the left there was a nice field there: we used to play ball up there. It was some beautiful up there.

I used to play ball on Broadway between the Tarr school (*the remainder of the old cotton mill, now the town library*) and Dock Square: the big hitters used to hit the Thurston & Hale store on the corner of T Wharf. The real big hitters could hit it right over the roof. Webster's Field on Nugent's Stretch was way before my time. I used to pitch (a lefthander); I pitched for the Town Team a little.

There used to be a lot of ponds where they cut ice in the old days. Stimson's at the end of Pleasant Street was perhaps the biggest, and Charlie Lane had an ice pond down by the cranberry bog and Reuben Norwood had two ice houses at Mill Pond: one at the foot of the Mill Lane hill coming down to the pond and another over on the other side in back of Bob Anderson's place. Reuben was an ugly old bastard. Guys who needed work would ask Reuben when he was going to cut ice and he'd talk around his cigar and growl out, "Reuben will cut when Reuben is ready!" He didn't even want you to go down through Mill Lane; he lived on Mill Lane. Reuben's descendants lived on the Lane for years.

I think Fred Stimson, the guy who had an icehouse on Stimson's Pond, was a colonel in the Union Army and after one Civil War battle somewhere down South he saw this little colored boy on the battlefield. He struck up a conversation with him and wound up bringing him back to Rockport. This was Washington "Washy" Davis. Washy didn't know how old he really was but he used to play with my grandfather and when someone would ask him how old he was he'd say to ask Ben Tarr: that he had played with Ben Tarr when he was a kid and they were the same age. I used to help put the American Legion flags around in the cemetery and I told Arthur Erickson that we ought to put a flag on Washy Davis's grave. After all, he came up here with a Civil War veteran, so I put a flag on there and after that Dave Burgess put a flag there. I don't believe anyone does that now. Washy Davis used to live in the first house on the right on Spring Lane going up from Pleasant Street. To my knowledge Washy never was a ward of the town or state, he survived somehow. Stimson built that house for him and he lived there until he died. I can remember when he died: I must have been fourteen or fifteen years old. (*Washington Davis is buried in the same gravesite next to his mentor Fred Stimson in Rockport's Beechgrove cemetery at the end of Pleasant Street.*)

There was one guy I grew up with whose mother died some time ago and for one reason or another he couldn't make it back to town to supervise her burial so he asked a Rockport buddy to take care of things for him and he'd be home for the funeral if he could. His pal asked the grave digger (who drank a little) to put her in their family plot and the digger said there was no problem. They had the funeral, the fella showed up and discovered that his mother had been buried in someone elses lot. When he was asked if he wanted her reburied he said, hell no, leave her there, it's as good a place as any.

I married Mary (*the former Mary Somers*) in 1935 and some said we wouldn't be married a month but we've been married for 63 years: we fooled 'em. When we were first married I worked on the WPA* then in 1940 I went over to the Cape Ann Tool Company in the Cove. I worked on a hammer. With the war coming and all we worked three shifts; busy day and night. We used to shift around every two weeks; 8am to 4pm, 4pm to 12 midnight, and midnight to 8 in the morning. I didn't mind shifting; I fell asleep all right. Some of the guys would say, I can't sleep, I can't sleep. I worked there from 1940 to 1978. On those hot summer days we'd go home for lunch to get out of that heat for a little while. . .some guys would work right through.

We got paid piece work and when the price was right we made damn good money. On other stuff we hardly made a cent: it all depended on what the Company got for the forgings. They wouldn't put it up, they were hard. But maybe they weren't making much. We had different scales for different products: we used different kinds of steel and that figured in. Some of it was hard to heat: you had to be awful careful with stainless: if it wasn't heated just so it would break up in little pieces.

I think that if Edith Dean (*the last owner of the Tool Company*) had lived longer she would have given the town that Pigeon Cove wharf.** I probably could have made more money up at the Shoe or GE but I didn't want that commute. I didn't want to ride up to Beverly and Lynn.

I had cancer of the esophagus when I was 75. That's bad stuff; you can have it and not know it and by the time you do know it it's in your stomach and you're done. I was

*Works Progress Administration: a Federal work program during the Great Depression.
**Sparing the town the resulting trauma between the Tool Company inheritors and the Pigeon Cove lobstermen and fishermen that erupted when the heirs wanted to sell off the Tool Company and the wharf. After a long bargaining process the wharf is currently owned by the Pigeon Cove Boatowners Association and negotiations are under way for the Town to take it over.

The end of Tuna Wharf, the Motif's sister pier. In the foreground is a typical open lobster boat common to that earlier time: no superstructure and no winches on these small craft.

up at Mass General and they operated on me and they got halfway through and the guy said he wondered if he had got enough of it out, so they stopped and opened me up again, I was seven hours on the operating table. I never had any radiation or anything and was up there for a week and a half or so and came home: no radiation or chemotherapy. I never went back to the hospital again.

ELIZABETH WILSON ENGEL

Born: 1924. Betty grew up in Rockport, married Ted Engel and lived in Needham for 39 years before moving back and continues to live in her home town. They have three children, the oldest child was born in Germany, two of whom are twins; they were born in Boston. Just because she lived off Cape for so long does not mean that Betty forgot her roots.

MY MOTHER WAS Maude Gott. She was a direct descendant of the first settler of Rockport. Her father was Chester Gott. Her mother was born in Lunenberg, Nova Scotia: I think her family was from Scotland. The famous Rockport artist, Lester Stevens, was in my mother's Rockport high school graduating class.

In the winter months Chester built and repaired small boats in the cellar of his home at 10 Gott Street. He built larger boats in his barn next door, which he later sold to artist Howard Smith who made it into two artists studios which he rented out in the summers. Stanley Woodward rented one of them for a time, After that it was renovated into a home owned by Max Kuehne. Chester was a lobsterman and had the first fish house on "Star Island" off Atlantic Avenue. He was Rockport harbor master for nearly 50 years and according to Ned Cameron was the first to shuttle tourists out to Thachers Island. I spent a lot of evenings with my grandfather listening to *The Lone Ranger*. He had one of those round-oval shaped radios but could receive the Lone Ranger direct from Chicago onWORL or some such call letters. When my grandfather died my mother inherited his house at 10 Gott Street and we moved in there and did some extensive renovations. My father was born in Rockport.

His name was A. Victor "Vic" Wilson and he was a letter carrier in Rockport for fifty years. His mother's name was Joannah and I think she was born in Rockport. His father was born in Sweden and the Swedish family name was Wilhelmson which I believe means the son of William. It became shortened to Wilson either over there or at Ellis Island. He got an award from Washington in recognition of his long and dedicated 50 years of service. In those days there were two mail deliveries each day. He walked and walked. I believe an article about his years of service calculated that he had walked 150,000 miles. After I stopped riding my bicycle he'd ride it to the Post Office and back home to save some walking.

My father was also secretary-treasurer of the Rockport Social Club which had a meeting place on Main Street up over the early Rockport National Bank. The club was a male gathering spot with such members as Lindley Dean, Arthur Swanson, Frank Pierce and other Rockport luminaries. It was said that many of the members were top bridge players, my father being one of them. He wouldn't play bridge with me; I wasn't good enough!

I had an older sister, Eleanor, who married "Dyke" Brown. Eleanor was a school teacher and first had a nursery school in her home before that. She also substituted in the Rockport schools. I had her one day which didn't make me very happy. I told her not to pick on any of my friends. She ended up teaching about twenty five years in the Gloucester school system. After I was married and older we became very good friends and developed strong family ties.

I grew up at 40 School Street, in one of

the two side by side houses that were known as "company houses" and are still standing. At that time they were owned by Mabel Woodfall (*the former long-time town librarian*). There was a big field in back of the houses and the Balzarini family would come from the Cove and do the haying in June and September. The Balzarinis also delivered our milk. One day a friend and I accidentally set the field on fire and they had to call out the fire department to put out the fire.

One of my best neighborhood friends growing up was Florence Heald: Florence Louise Heald Ames now. She lived on School Street toward High Street. Art Rich lived around the corner on High Street. We used to play hide and seek and kick the can in the back yards of our respective houses: in back they all sort of ran together. Jack Reilly from up on Summer Street used to join us. Johnny Pierce lived on Pleasant Street and he was part of our neighborhood crowd.

We had a crowd that sort of hung out together. We had a lot of fun in those days: our friends spanned three grades. There was Bea DeCosta, Ginger Fritz and Phylis Perkins from the class behind me, Nancy Wickey, Norma Leavitt, Margie Norton from our class and once in a while Ruth Fritz, Ginger's older sister.

When we had the high school band we'd get together after practice and have jam sessions: I played the trumpet. The band was started by Herm Erwin when I was a freshman. The band was a big event in Rockport, especially in the Memorial Day parade. We were asked to play in Gloucester at the Our Lady of Good Voyage church and gave concerts to proud parents and friends and neighbors. All that

was necessary for the bands success was one good player for the trumpets, trombones, clarinets and drums and the rest of us supplied the background. Herm Erwin was a real asset to the schools and to the town. As everyone knows, he owned and ran the Peg Leg Restaurant for years. Many years after high school I had dinner at the Peg Leg and he greeted me with, "How's your lip?"

We went for walks in the woods around Devil's Den and Spruce Hut and I loved to pick blueberries. I went blueberrying with my father a lot. He used to go berrying up near Briar Swamp but I never went there with him. We used to go through Nugent's piggery on Sundays in August for our berries in a swampy area. I was a finicky picker, my berries were always clean. My mother hated to go over my father's berries because he'd have a can around his waist and pick with two hands: just shovel them in, red ones, green ones and stems all together.

I took some art lessons from May Bennett Brown when I was real young: twenty five cents a lesson. I've always had an interest in art. I've taken art lessons over the years from Rockport's greatest but I've remained the same: just interested. I've got a picture somewhere I took of Stanley Woodward and Anthony Thieme standing next to each other. I also worked in the Blacksmith Shop bakery on Main Street in the summers when I was going to school in Boston.

I never went out for team sports but I've always loved to ski. Art Rich made some innovative bindings for my skis from old inner tubes; preludes to ski bindings. I used to go up on Pigeon Hill and ski. We used to ski in BeechGrove cemetery down between the grave lots to the wall above Stimson's Pond and ice house. If you couldn't or didn't turn, over the wall you went, a six foot drop.

There always seemed enough for us to do even though I read in the papers these days that the young people complain that there's no place for them to hang out. There seems to be a need for more team sports. We walked a lot: we walked everywhere and that took some time out of our days. I remember gathering at Bea DeCosta's home on Broadway in the center part of town (*where the present Granite Savings Bank is located*) and we'd play games, play the piano and clown around: it was a natural gathering spot and maybe a gathering place is needed today.

When we were growing up here we related to older people: real old people, from the grandparents age group. It wasn't just family you associated with, it was the whole neighborhood, no matter how old some might have been. Our neighborhood was comprised of a lot of older people but I thought that was great. They were very nice to me and I liked them. Now that I'm much older I love having younger people in the area. I don't think we have that much of a mix of older and younger people in neighborhoods nowadays.

We had the Tufts's on School Street and their greenhouse next door to 10 Gott Street. The Tufts girls had the CandleTree tea shop at one time on the corner of School and High Street: they owned that whole complex there. The Tufts treated me very kindly; as if I was a good little kid. I always went into their greenhouse and talked with them (they treated me like I was older than I was). Maybe it was the beginning of my interest in gardening.

Esther Longley lived in an apartment on the corner of Gott and School Street. I took piano lessons from her for either 25 or 50 cents. Down along Gott Street was Mrs. Jules Jeppson. She used to make her Swedish coffee rolls for my sister and she finally realized that I liked them too. When she sent them up after that she said they were for both of us.

I wish young people today could have a life like we did when we grew up: neighborly, friendly, open, safe and few if any restrictions. I suppose life then was easier to be good than it is for kids growing up today. We had competitiveness back then but I think the stress is much greater now. We have a lot more mechnical gadgets now but it's not all that good. There's a lot more violence.

When I'm asked to describe the good and the bad about growing up in Rockport I can't find anything bad. My husband Ted says he would have given anything to have been brought up in Rockport. He grew up in Queens, New York and moved to Newton, Mass. after his sophomore year of high school and graduated from Newton High. He has said the greatest gift anyone could have would be to have grown up in Rockport.

Ted had to serve two years in the Army after he graduated from dental school. We first lived in Fort Knox, Kentucky. I've said that I escaped from Fort Knox with their gold: I had two gold-inlay fillings while there. He was transferred from there during the Korean War to France. I joined him for a year. Our oldest child was born in Landstuhl, Germany in the new Army General Hospital. That hospital is often in the news: the place where Army personnel is checked out before returning to the

States.

If I had been asked when I was fifteen or sixteen what I would change about Rockport I might have said some things about the school department. Maybe I wouldn't have been as kind toward some of my teachers as I am now. But the farther away you get from that time it doesn't seem that things were so bad after all.

In our senior high school class yearbooks (*Rocks and Pebbles*) it said I wanted to see the world and I guess I've seen a good portion of it. We had our fiftieth reunion recently and Dewey Olson asked me to keep the old class records because he thinks I like to save things. I've always wondered how Dewey knew this about me.

I went on to the Boston University College of Practical Arts and Letters after high school. My father believed in further education. I ended up being a private secretary at the Godfrey Cabot Corporation in Boston: now just the Cabot Corporation. I commuted to Boston on the Boston and Maine and my father usually picked me up at the train station. I didn't get home until about seven o'clock. Back then the main meal was at noon for those who worked in town. My mother always had a meal ready for me, she cooked two dinner meals a day. (Edith Mills was a neighbor and we commuted together; she worked for an insurance company in Boston.)

When Ted and I were first married he still had two more years of dental school. We lived on Beacon Hill and I thought it was the greatest to walk to work through Boston Common but I'm not sure it's the thing to do today.

As far as changes in the world since I grew up in Rockport there has been a lot of progress and progress, for the most part, is good. There's been an awful lot of progress in the medical field. As far as a philosophy of life goes there still seems to be something lacking. There's such an emphasis on bad news these days: all you hear about is killings. It's not the easiest world to bring up children in. I'm concerned nowadays about my grandchildren and how they'll cope with the drug scene. It takes a very strong fifteen or sixteen year old to say no to all the people they associate with. Maybe it's a fear of being isolated: so many of them seem to go along with the flow. As a child you always want to be liked, to be a member of a group. We tell them to pick their friends but I don't know how many choices they have.

As we get older we find we have a lot of unfinished projects or goals, due to the fact that it takes us twice as long to do half as much. Sometimes I wonder why I continue thinking the way I do, at my age, as if I was thirty or forty years old. I still cut out recipes from magazines and say why am I still doing this? I feel that my mind is willing but my body is having trouble catching up. My mother used to say that growing old is a privilige denied to many. I've begun to think of a lot things my mother used to say.

I think anybody can have a physical ailment, give up and sit in a chair and feel sorry for themselves (*Betty has a bad back which would incapacitate many others*). You play the cards dealt to you and do the best you can. I don't see life ending for quite a while. On balance, getting older is more positive than negative: I still have a lust for life.

I think I'd like to be remembered as having been able to brighten someone's day, to have made them smile. I like to think there's some good in everyone. I'm always having coffee and doughnuts so I'll probably be remembered as much for that as anything else. Or it's possible that some will remember me for my gardening. Since childhood I've always been weeding gardens, edging grass, cutting dead blossoms. My mother *never* had me do housework. . .but I enjoyed taking care of her gardens and yard.

A "Star Island" fish shack. Note the old oak slatted lobster traps and hanging buoys which marked where the traps were set when fishing.

ELIZABETH ELSO GRAHAM

Betty was born in the house at 14 King Street in Rockport on June 5, 1921, making her a true Rockport native. She lived, with her early Elso family, in a number of places in Rockport and Pigeon Cove over the years. After graduating from Rockport High School she went to the Mary Brooks School in Boston; an institution specializing in teaching secretarial and book keeping skills. At one time Betty served as secretary to the famous frozen food innovator, Clarence Birdseye at his home in East Gloucester. This job was followed by a much longer stint with the Frank E. Davis Fish Company in Gloucester. Betty still does some free-lancing book keeping. "My husband Bob and I had two girls. He's gone now but I have five grandchildren and seven great-grandchildren to keep me busy."

M Y MOTHER AND FATHER were six and seven years old when they came to this country with their parents from Finland. They came over in about 1893. In those days the men came over first and the women and children followed. Both of my grandfathers came to this country before their wives.

My grandfather Hendrickson and his brother went to Hurricane Island in Maine directly from Finland. He was in granite work up there. My grandfather Elso started out in Ashtabula, Ohio but I'm not sure what he did there. The Hendricksons came from Oulu and the Elsos came from Vaasa in Finland: Oulo was in northern Finland and Vaasa was in the southern part. After my grandmother Hendrickson came to this country she and my grandfather moved to Rockport. Both of my grandfathers worked in the granite quarries: the quarries may have been what drew them here in the first

place. They both died of what was called consumption in those days but probably was the awful, all too well known, early quarry workers disease, "white lung" from all the granite dust they breathed in when they worked the stone. No masks or safety glasses in those days.

(At this point in our conversation I wondered aloud if perhaps her grandfathers had, like my own grandfather, come to this country to avoid conscription into the the Czarist army, Finland being, at the time the Duchy of Finland, a part of the Russian empire. Service in the Russian military was more often than not a death sentence. Betty allowed as how that may well have been true.)

The Hendricksons came to Pigeon Cove and I believe lived upstairs over the school house on the corner of Phillips Avenue and Green Street. *(The building still stands opposite the Emerson Inn, but is now a private residence even though Pigeon Cove elders still call it the old school house.)* They actually moved back and forth between Rockport and Pigeon Cove, always renting. Quarry workers couldn't buy a house; they weren't paid enough. They moved around a lot, even though they didn't ever leave Rockport or Pigeon Cove. They lived there on the Avenue, behind a livery stable in Dock Square in Rockport, on Pigeon Hill Street and Curtis Street in the Cove, and on the corner of Forest and Granite Streets among many other locations.

My mother never went beyond the third grade in school. This happened because when my mother and her brother and family moved from Rockport to Pigeon Cove they were sent back to the first grade. Nobody had bothered to check their school records in Rockport to see if they had indeed been in school there. When they moved back to Rockport they had to start all over once again in the first grade. (*A classic example of how some minorities were once treated in early Rockport. An unpleasant memory in these days of assimilation.*)

My mother started working at age thirteen; the family needed income so she couldn't go to school any more. She worked as a house maid for a Newcombe family, who owned a lobster company in town and lived in a pretty large house atop the rise across from Front Beach next to the Fifth Parish Cemetery, the present site of the Peg Leg Motel. At one time she worked for Doctor Tupper on Main Street in that large house next to the Congregational Church: she did housework for everybody and his uncle. She also cared for sick people and eventually became a midwife.

When my grandfather Hendrickson came to this country his last name was spelled Pyy in Finnish. The name was pronounced sort of like Buuh (the B's and P's sounds in Finnish are alike. The Americans can't seem to make their mouths and lips do that.) When he went to work for the Rockport Granite Company they said they couldn't pronounce his name and asked him what his father's name had been. He said Hendrick, so they called him Hendrick's son and that's how that name became Hendrickson. And as long as we're talking about pronounciation, one thing that gripes me is how a lot of people pronounce sauna as "sawnah" when all Finns know that it's said as "sownah."

I don't know where my grandparents Elso lived at first but they eventually bought a house on what we used to call Pig Street, Norwood Court now. This was a short sort of

lane that ran along behind the Back Beach side of Forest Street. I guess the place got that name because some of the Finns in the area raised pigs there. Forest Street is still called Finn Alley by many old timers because of all the Finns who used to live on it. Most of the kids on Forest Street were Finns. There were two Finn markets, a Finnish Lutheran church and a Temperance Hall on that one short street.

At one time we moved over to Main Street in the main part of town. We took some ribbing because we were Finnish and had the nerve to move to Main Street, but that never bothered me. I never let it bother me that there were people in town who thought that because I was a Finn I was something less than they were. I remember when my mother was working for forty cents an hour and she came home one day and said that the women were going to start charging sixty cents an hour for their labor, but she wasn't going to do it. I was only little at the time and asked her why she wasn't going to do it. She said she couldn't charge that much and I said to her that the people she worked for had more money than she had. I don't know if my comment had anything to do with it but she went along with the sixty cents an hour charge for housework.

My mother made all our clothes. She would alter clothes handed over from some of the people she worked for and said that by the time she got through with them they were better than any clothes she could buy. And she was right.

My Hendrickson grandparents lived for a time in the first house on the right as you go up Paddy Hill (*a section that got its name from the Irish quarry workers who onced lived along there*). Paddy Hill is that rise between what is now known as the Rowe Point condominiums and the keystone bridge.

Those houses along that stretch were called Company houses at one time: Granite Company houses for employees. My grandmother Hendrickson had six kids at the time and they took in six borders. I don't know how they did it. My mother was the oldest of the kids: my grandmother Hendrickson had come over with two kids; my mother and my uncle Henry. She was seven and Henry was six. Henry wound up working at the Cape Ann Tool Company. My grandmother had thirteen kids all told: of course, only seven of them lived to be adults.

My father worked on the William H. Moody*, the Rockport Granite Company steam lighter, going back and forth to New York. He went from that job to the Tool Company. While working there he got a piece of metal in his eye and had to go to Boston to have it fixed. They removed the piece but did something too early and he lost sight in that eye. He had the eye but couldn't see out of it. He could stand on top of Pigeon Hill and look at the town clock with his one eye and tell you what time it was. After he left the Tool Company he went to the WPA. My father went to work for Gorton Pew in Gloucester for a time after the WPA and wound up as stationary engineer at the Addison Gilbert Hospital, keeping the heating system going because he had earned those papers. My father died at 76 but my mother lived to be 90.

To me the Depression was just another year: you heard stories but it didn't bother me because we were poor to begin with. My mother went back to work doing housework while my father got $13.50 a week from WPA work. She used to cook down at the Rockport Country Club and at the Straitsmouth Inn near Gap Head in the South End. We used to call the Straitsmouth Inn the black hotel because from Front Beach all those old shingles looked as if they were black.

Mrs. Louis Rogers was the wife of the owner of the Rockport Granite Company and one of my mother's employers. I worked for them also and even though Louie was thought of as a not very nice person, I liked him better than I liked her. But she did give us free passes to go to the movies in Gloucester so we were able to go to the movies twice a week and pay only bus fare. Someone (we still don't know who) turned us in and said we were going to the movies all the time while my father worked for the WPA.** I suppose whoever turned us in thought we were making some money on the side: money we weren't supposed to have with my father on the WPA. My mother refused to turn the passes in to the WPA clerk, telling her that they were given to her by the lady she worked for and we only paid bus fare to go to the movies. The WPA lady said that my sister and I were also well dressed (as if that was a crime) and my mother said that was right because we wore other people's leftovers and that she did also. So the woman finally said that if she could do that then she should please enjoy the passes. We never did find out who had turned us in. It might have been one of our neighbors for all we knew.

*The authors' father, Captain Roger H. Martin Sr., first went seriously to sea aboard the William H. Moody.
**Standout local results from the WPA projects are the combination police and fire station on Broadway and the grandstand at Evans Field

You know, I didn't talk English until I was five years old. We lived over on Main Street (#85) and a family with two young girls lived upstairs over us. They came downstairs and asked if I wanted to play with them. My mother said it was OK with her but she didn't know how we'd understand each other. In a matter of weeks I was talking English and that gave me a head start on English before going to school. I don't remember any language problems in school so I must have learned well from the girls upstairs. Those of us Finns who had older brothers and sisters also got a head start from what they had already learned and relayed to us at home.

When I was a sophomore in high school we moved to Pigeon Cove and we thought we had moved to the end of the world. Some of us got passes to go to school in Rockport on the bus but sometimes a kid could live right across the street from someone who got a pass and they'd have to walk over a mile to school. We lived at number thirty three Pigeon Hill Street *(the former old Sheep Pasture)* and everybody around there was either Finn or Swede. There used to be a Swedish church across the street from our house. That church was moved later on over to Stockholm Avenue. They did a lot of house moving way back. Down on the corner was the store run by the blind man, Mr. Erickson. He was blinded in the quarries. We used to go there to buy a lot of things: bread, coffee and like that. He ran the store on the honor system. The store was connected to the house and his wife was there if he needed help, but he seldom asked for it. Nobody would cheat him.

We'd try every once in a while to get our parents to talk about coming over from Finland but they were so young at the time that they didn't have very strong memories. My father loved Rockport: he was always talking about the wonders of Rockport. Both my mother and father were naturalized and later on helped other Finns to study for their naturalization and even go up with them to Boston for the test. One time I had to go along because my father couldn't go, with a certain Finn from Pigeon Cove when he went before the judges to get his papers. He was a drinker. When we got in front of the judges one of them asked him if he had ever been arrested. He said yes: for booze. They had a good laugh over that. When we got out this man gave us train fare home and said he had an errand to attend to and he'd see us later. My mother said, "Yah, I betchya, some errand!" and said she'd bet he'd come home drunk that night. I used to hear that there are two kinds of Finns: drunks and non-drunks.

View of Star Island fish shacks across the harbor toward Bearskin Neck. If you look closely you can spot the old Coast Guard double ender surf boat at her mooring. These shacks were washed off their perches some years ago.

THE HOOPER SCHOOL STREET GATHERING

This event was a session of an open and variable group which met nearly every weekday at Abbot Hooper's house on School Street at four in the afternoon beginning in 1990 and continued on a regular basis until 2000. The conversation was wide open and unpredictable but usually centered on the Rockport they all remembered. One of the more interesting aspects of this daily gathering of Rockport natives was that they put no conditions on who joined in: even to including some relative newcomers like John Krenn. All that was asked for and ascertained (just how was a mystery) was that anyone attending must have the best interests of the town at heart. This transcript may seem disjointed but it does reflect the free-wheeling discussions that erupted nearly every day. Each day's meeting was terminated at precisely five o'clock, sometimes in the middle of a sentence, so Ab could get his supper in time. This transcript (somewhat edited) typifies what transpired every day during that ten year period at Ab's place on School Street: a prime source for sometimes inexact reminiscences but never without interest, controversy or good humor.

Those present when I visited them on a March day in 1997 were: Dr. Abbott Hooper, born 1915, retired dentist who served Cape Ann for many years. Lewis Norwood, born 1916, formerly with the U. S. Dept. of Agriculture. Story Parsons, born 1915, retired from the U. S. Post Office railway mail service. Ben Hull, born 1916, retired Mass. Electric. Carl Lovgren, born 1919, retired from the "industrial scene". On this day all of those present grew up in Rockport. Since this transcript was made Ben Hull and Story Parsons have died, and at this writing (2001) Ab Hooper is resident in the Den Mar Nursing facility and Lovgren and Norwood are at home.

HULL: The only car we had in high school was Betty Marshall's.

NORWOOD: The Marshall's lived next to the Broadway school: a little small house.
HULL: They lived in a white house by Five Corners.

NORWOOD: No. No. No.

HOOPER: This happens every day: we'll throw out a fact and nobody can remember it. Then we'll argue about where so and so lived: no, he lived there, he didn't live here, he lived there.

PARSONS: Betty used to run around with Al Holgerson: I can remember them walking up Broadway and her mother used to be with them. They must have lived up there someplace.

LOVGREN: They used to live where old Cap Green lived years ago. (*Cap Green ran a pool hall in Dock Square and lived at Five Corners*).

NORWOOD: Who remembers who used to work for Cap Green? It was my uncle, good old Pomp Silva. He'd slip me a bar of candy once in a while.

HULL: There'd be days when Cap's place was full and he'd kick everyone out; tell 'em to go on home. There'd be other days when he wasn't making a nickel but he'd stay open all day long. Years ago we convinced Cap to run for selectman, told him he was a shoo-in. Well, anyway, he wound up with forty votes. He said, "You bunch of Goddamn liars!"

PARSONS: We used to play pool there on Cap's table: it had big pockets so the game would go quick. I think those pockets were twice as big as the ones I got on my table.

LOVGREN: Cap was one of the reasons they probably voted out booze in town.

NORWOOD: Including my uncle Pomp.

HULL: I used to buy my hot dogs at Cap's; they were fifteen cents, I loved that.

LOVGREN: Cap had beer there and Bill MacDonald had it too, for a while.

(MARTIN: *All you guys played baseball when you were young didn't you?*)

HULL: Not all of us, but Lew hit a single once off Johnny Lamb. (*Johnny Lamb was arguably the best pitcher ever to play baseball in Rockport*)

NORWOOD: It was a home run! Nobody believes it but it was.

HULL: You couldn't hit him if he come in and tossed it to you.

NORWOOD: It was true that the outfield was playing in, close to shortstop. I got a hold of one and I also hit one in Essex that hit the town hall up there.

HULL: Nobody could hit Lambie . . . his curve was so sharp I thought he was going to hit me in the head with it.

NORWOOD: Ben (*Hull*) played second

base: went two seasons without making an error.

PARSONS: He never went after anything more than five feet away.

HULL: The greatest one for something like that was Solly Thurston: every move Solly made, it meant something. No wasted effort, he was slow but he was there.

PARSONS: I asked Solly Thurston once who was the best pitcher he ever faced and he said without any doubt, it was Johnny Lamb.

HULL: Johnny Lamb, to my mind, was the best pitcher in this area: that includes Gloucester, Manchester and all around here. (*Lamb pitched for teams as far away as New Hampshire in his prime: twenty five dollars a game.*)

HULL: I see Ann Fisk is having an exhibit somewhere.

HOOPER: Is she painting in watercolors now? I saw her down at the RAA (*Rockport Art Association*) one day and she said she was practising with oils.

(MARTIN: *My wife and I saw Ann one day recently, painting in oils (I could smell them) at that cemetery across from Front Beach. Does that cemetery have a name?*)

HOOPER: That's the Sandy Bay Cemetery. . . First Parish Cemetery. . .named when we were part of Gloucester. (*It is actually the Fifth Parish Cemetery, Sandy Bay being the Fifth Gloucester Parish before opting for independence.*)

NORWOOD: And who else is up in there?

HOOPER: Hannah Jumper (*Leader of the famous Rockport housewives liquor raid*)

PARSONS: I went down there and cleaned off that stone so you could read it. It was slow work but I cleaned it off with almost clear Clorox. It wasn't one of those slate ones, some kind of stone or composition.

(*Here the talk shifts to art: primarily local art and artists*)

HULL: Some of the those old artists are starting to sell pretty good nowadays.

PARSONS: What gets me are the prices some of these artists are getting. I get a weekly paper about auctions, etc. and there was a Cecil Chichester; he painted around here: Burkey had any number of them over there. I could have bought any amount for ten or fifteen dollars apiece. And a Cecil Chichester the other day brought three thousand dollars. He painted here but I don't think he lived here. There's another one, Albert Insley. I think his stuff is crap but it's bringing in a few bucks. There was another painter: Harvey. His stuff could be found all over the country for ten or fifteen dollars. When they got as high as seventy five dollars old Bill Hoyt stopped buying them: too high a price. Hoyt must have thirty or forty of his works. We did find a couple of good ones. (*The "we" a reference to the Sandy Bay Historical Society, which Bill Hoyt curated for many years and to which Hoyt left much of his estate, including many paintings.*)

NORWOOD: I bought two Tucker Margesons when I graduated from college for twenty five dollars apiece. Tucker was one of my paper customers.

PARSONS: Way back in high school I started collecting paintings when I could get a few bucks and Tucker gave me one. He knew I was starting in and he gave me one. He told me the first time I got a chance to get one by Aldro Hibbard because he's the best in the world on snow. It was a long time before I got one but I did, I got three of them.

HULL: I got two little Margesons when I was married.

PARSONS: I remember way, way back when his painting was so very fine and then he got broad: still good but a different style. You don't see many of those early ones. Originally he was pretty tight. You go to these auctions and it's unbelievable: they buy the name. Emile Gruppe is one: I see some of his stuff go for big money and it's crap. He did a lot of good work. I saw one of his large landscapes one time out in New York and thought the auctioneer might get 25, 30 thousand for it but I saw another one and told him he'd better take what he could get for it. It think he got 28 thousand for that big one. . .the other one he got nine hundred for and I told him he did well. I waited a long time to get a Gruppe that I liked and finally got one down at an auction in Florida and got it for three thousand dollars. I got some good Margesons. You know, between 1880 and 1920 he did some great work. And all his good ones are signed and dated. About 1920 he began to go downhill and didn't do much after that. He was a nice man.

LOVGREN: He did those big paintings in Brown's Department Store (*in Gloucester*).

PARSONS: Margeson did two big paintings that you saw when you looked down that big main staircase and probably got nil for doing them and I've got one of them.

(MARTIN: *Where do you store your paintings: do you hang them all?*)

PARSONS: I got them hanging: I've got about seventy five of them. I can't hang many more. I understand you (*Martin*) used to be good before you went modern: ship paintings.

(MARTIN: *Yes, I painted ships and sometimes sold them literally wet off the easel: but I got tired of doing them.*)

PARSONS: Yes, I can understand that.

HOOPER: Tucker Margeson came to this town as a telegraph operator.

PARSONS: He did that. He had a little store down there; sold stationary supplies and took messages. Right down on Main Street somewhere.

HULL: Is Gil Emery (*Margeson's step-son*) still alive?

PARSONS: Last I knew he's in New Hampshire. Years ago I saw him up there. He was still painting and doing some nice watercolors. Years ago he did a few oils and they were good, but in those days he could-

n't get enough money to buy oils.

HULL: I buy what I like. Some people go for the name before they'll hang it in their living room. I've seen some of it and it's horse-shit art. I buy what I like.

HOOPER: Everything (*art*) in this room has an emotional value to me.

(*At this point the conversation once again shifted, which, from what I gathered is rather the rule than the exception*)

NORWOOD: You know who's got a lot of stories, particularly about Everett Sanborn, is Bud Curtis. The one I like the most was when Everett was at Den Mar (had diabetes and all) and he was walking down town on a cold, sloppy day and this woman, apparently a nurse, saw him and stopped and said come on Everett, get in, I don't want you walking around in this weather. She got him out of the car and said "Now look Everett, I'm going to help you but I don't want you to slip down and fall on top of me." To which Everett replied; "I couldn't be that lucky."

LOVGREN: Tell about what he said about Tarr and Marr. (*A former Rockport real estate firm noted for their ability to strike deals advantageous to their company*)

NORWOOD: People come from near and far to be screwed by Tarr and Marr.

(MARTIN: *The best Sanborn story I've heard was Everett's comment to a surgeon prior to surgery. The doctor asked him what he did for a living. Everett (who at the time worked on the cemetery crew) replied that he buried the doc-*

tor's mistakes.)

HULL: I wonder who owns the Addison Gilbert now: Beverly or Cape Ann. They've got a lot of good art there and I wonder who owns it now *(after the merger between the AGH and Beverly Hospital).*

PARSONS: They've got a lot of good paintings there.

(MARTIN: Here I come to this gang of old Rockporters and the main topic is art. Totally unexpected. There's something about growing up in this town that did us all a world of good. I can't put my finger on it.)

HULL: Marion Marshall did a lot of good for us as a teacher.

LOVGREN: Ma Hathaway was a good teacher. I don't know; I think she taught ancient history: American history. She was forever telling us about the great artists of the world. She spent a lot of time on great art.

PARSONS: She was a great teacher. We didn't appreciate her. I wish some of these Johnny-come-latelies who want to change everything around would appreciate what the town was. They get in here and think it's great and then they want to change everything.

HOOPER: There are people around who want to make the town work.

(MARTIN: I've always thought of you, Ab, as a very sympathetic person. You can carry that too far Ab. (general laughter). You can't forgive everybody.)

PARSONS: Hey, that's pretty well put.

HULL: Well, Goddamn it, you're the Poet Laureate, you ought to come up with something sharp. I tell you about good teachers in my day: Catherine Churchill, I never had her but she was a good one. Martha Mansfield was a good teacher. . .Marty Mansfield's mother. And Margaret O'Connor: Maggie O'Connor. She taught me to type; the only Goddamn thing I can remember. Margaret Higgins was another one.

At this point it was five o'clock, the exact time for the group to break up, no matter what or where any conversation might be. Carl Lovgren is the unofficial timekeeper and has been known to interrupt someone in the middle of a sentence to make his announcement.

After the visit described and recorded above I returned for a short one on one interview with Dr. Abbott Hooper. The following are his remarks during that interview.

A HOOPER WAS A MAN who made barrel hoops: those round metal bands that held the whole thing together. A woman in England told me that, and she seemed to be knowledgeable. But here in America most Hoopers were seamen. Most of them were fishermen but the rich ones were merchants. The King-Hooper mansion in Marblehead is named for a Hooper who was a merchant.

I think the original Rockport Hoopers came from Marblehead. The Hoopers started out in Cornwall in England: there's millions of Hoopers over there. I was over there one time and walked down the street and there's Hoopers all over the place. They first came to this country as fishermen and they went first to Marblehead.

It was said that the fishermen in Marblehead were so terrible and evil that they needed a minister. They recruited a minister from Newburyport and his name was Thacher. So he took his family and put 'em on a boat and headed for Marblehead. That's when they got caught in a storm and washed ashore on Thacher's Island. And I don't believe he ever did get to Marblehead. (*In Anthony Thacher's own account of his ordeal on the island he does say that on the Tuesday following the tragic shipwreck his wife and he finally arrived in Marblehead.*) The Hoopers were in Marblehead before the Revolution.

It was during the Revolution when one of them, I suppose this Hooper must have been a fisherman, met a girl in Gloucester and married her. Then along came the war and he went on, I suppose it was like a privateer (I think it was named the *Yankee*), and it was captured. He was taken to Dartmouth in Nova Scotia as a prisoner, where he died. But his pregnant wife went back to live with her family in Gloucester; that's how the Hoopers got to Cape Ann. I think his name was Robert. The Hoopers didn't have much imagination as far as names went: they had long lists of John, John, John, and Robert, Robert.

There was a Hooper in the Barbados. I don't know just what the relationship was but this Hooper was probably a rum merchant. That Barbados rum is good rum. When they got to Cape Ann they became carpenters. There was one of 'em, either John or Robert, who's buried here in Beech Grove cemetery.

And then, of course, there was the John who had the lumber yard. He was the great, great, great, ever so great John who, I think, built the house on the corner of Mill Lane and Main Street. Now, the John Hooper* who always wore four hats was my grandfather and his father was John Hooper the first, who was a lumber dealer on Mill Lane. His business was responsible for the Bearskin wharf being named Lumber Wharf. He would have lumber sent probably from Maine I suppose, and unload it on that wharf (*part of what we used to call White Wharf*) and then dray it up to that Mill Lane barn where he stored it. Napoleon Setti (*a stained glass artist who had his studio in that barn many years later*) told me that the marks from dragging the lumber were still on the floors. Later on, many artists used that building for studios: Lester Stevens and Maurice Compris, among others.

My father worked all his life at the Rockport Granite Company. He was the bookkeeper. I suppose in keeping with his trade, he had to be well-dressed. When I was little he used to ride his bicycle to work. It wasn't until I was a bit older that he got an automobile: I think it was Model T Ford.

I started my practice with Earl Andrews in Gloucester because I was afraid nobody'd come to me because they knew me as a little boy and they'd say, well, he can't know anything about dentistry. So I started out on my own in Gloucester in that building the bank has now as their trust department. After that I went into the military service: I hadn't been in practice all that long. I went into the Navy as a dentist. They drafted me as a

---

*(This was the famous Johnny Hooper who spent his life driving his horse and team around town dressed pretty much in rags and numbers of hats, but who left his heirs very well off when he died.)

dentist and my first station was down in Newport. We had to rent a room: there wasn't room for us on base. I've been retired since 1984.

As far as being remembered after I'm gone I find it awfully hard to step outside myself and say how I'd like to be remembered. I don't know how anybody could say that.

As I left Ab's house that day I mentioned in passing that he, Lew Norwood and myself had all lost our wives and that we could sympathize with Lew about his wife's recent death. I wondered if Ab had ever thought of getting remarried, thinking of my so fortunate remarriage to Ann Nichols O'Grady after Joan's death, and Ab paused and said very quietly, "I made up my mind when my wife died *(the former Ginnie Lovgren, Carl's sister)* I wasn't going to marry again. I was married to a wonderful wife and I didn't want to spoil it."

Two church steeples: the Universalist on the right and the Congregational on the left, framed by the old willow trees that once graced the shore at Back Beach.

CATHERINE PASCUCCI JULIAN

Born on Cape Ann in 1929. Catherine is the daughter of the one-time Rockport shoe maker and shoe repairman Joseph Pascucci, who was a Main Street fixture for many, many years, sitting in his sunny window, smiling and nodding at passersby, in the same space now occupied by his barber son-in-law Walter Julian, who has run the only old fashioned barbershop in town for the past 45 years. I chose to interview this rather unusually young (for the purpose of this oral history) Rockporter because of how much her father meant to generations of Rockporters, including the author. In my earlier book, Rockport Remembered, I recalled my fondness for Joe, saying, "I always felt a certain connection to Joe Pascucci as he sat in his shop window repairing shoes. Joe had the sweetest smile of any of the adults I knew."

JOSEPH PASCUCCI was born in 1883 in Bonito, Italy, a small hilltop town east of Naples, which gave onto an expansive view of the lower level town of Mirabella. This town was also the birthplace of the famous Italian designer, Ferragamo. Joseph was one of six children and came to the United States in 1906, following his two older brothers across the Atlantic. Joe's mother, Savaria (Sarah) DiChiara, convinced his father, Antonio to leave their bread and pasta business to go to America to be near their three sons. Two daughters and the youngest son came to America with their parents and settled in Framingham, Massachusetts.

Joe liked to explore the area north of Boston. During his travels he discovered Rockport when visiting one of his brothers who had chosen to live in Gloucester, and fell in love with the place. He came to town in 1912 and promptly opened his shoe repair business at 59 (now 53) Main Street (formerly Joe Thibeault's shop and lately an art gallery) and the town became his home for the rest of his life. In Italy Joe had learned to be a cobbler. To do this he had to pass a set of stringent tests, typified by one in which he was presented with some leather and told to make a pair of shoes. He was actually a shoemaker by training. In this he was like Ferragamo, who also was a shoemaker by education.

He met his wife, Caterina (Catherine) Spagnolo, when she and her family were visiting members of their family in Rockport. The Spagnolos did not intend to remain in this country but after Joe married Caterina in 1914 her family stayed in this country. In those days Italian parents wished to stay close to their children and that's just what the children wanted. . .to this day Italians have kept a strong sense of family.

Catherine was born in 1894 in Pedescala, a small village in northern Italy; north of Venice in the Venito region. She frequently commented on how fortunate she had been to have spent the first 20 years of her life in such a lovely place and the remaining 61 years of her life in Rockport: from a village looking up to the Italian Alps to an American seacoast village surrounded by the ocean.

Catherine had been engaged in Italy before she came to this country, and her fiance begged her not to go because he feared that if she went, she'd never come back. And then she met Joe in Rockport in May and was married to him in August: a whirlwind courtship in those days, but a marriage that lasted the rest of their lives.

She often said that she really couldn't refuse Joe, a Neapolitan, who was very emotional and a very loving person.

In 1916 Joe and Catherine bought their first house on High Street. In 1919, after the birth of their three sons, Anthony, John and Pasquale, Joe bought the 61-67 (now 55-57) Main Street building from Doctor Tupper, a well known and well loved local physician. Joe moved his business to this building where he remained until 1951. That building was sold to Walter Julian in 1967. Joe really did connect with young people and adored all children. He could be impatient with adults but children could do most anything. He also had a unique sense of humor.

This seldom noted sense of humor showed itself in different ways with different people. Jim Snow, one of Joe's shop "buddies" (men who stopped in to pass the time of day from time to time) once asked Joe to put new soles and heels on his shoes. When Jim picked them up, he told Joe to keep them because they were too tight and he never should have had them fixed. About a year later Jim came in looking for a pair of "used" shoes and Joe said he had just the right pair for him. Snow tried them on, stomped on the floor and said, "These are a perfect fit!" Jim asked how much he owed Joe and Joe figured out what the new soles and heels cost to put on the Snow shoes a year earlier and charged Jim accordingly. Snow never recognized his old shoes and when Joe finally told him about where they came from Jim couldn't and wouldn't believe him. This became one of Joe's favorite stories. Joe repaired countless pairs of shoes during the Depression, when there wasn't any money for such luxuries as new soles and heels.

My mother also had her own stories about her early days in Rockport. Both she and Joe used to laugh when Catherine would tell about the day a salesman came to the door of the 20 year old bride, who was still struggling with English, and attempted to sell her 5 pounds of macaroons for a given amount of money. Catherine responded indignantly (thinking the addled salesman couldn't even pronounce macaroni properly) and thought that he must think she was some fool to pay that much money for macaroni. She told him she could buy 20 pounds for that money.

My father used to love cars: he was a car aficionado. And my mother was one of the few women in Rockport to have a driver's license in 1920. Jennie Savage was another early woman driver in town. When you think about what my mother and father did here it's quite remarkable. These two came from another country not able to speak English. They came here and started from scratch, starting his business in 1912, got married in 1914, bought their first house by 1916, by 1917 they had three children: my brothers were all born a year apart and then I came along 12 years after my youngest brother. By 1919 they had bought the building on Main Street, bought their first car shortly after that, when there were only a few cars in town.

After we were married Walter and I lived in Brookline for a year; 1950. In 1951 we moved back to Rockport and have been here ever since. We had our son Joseph (named for my father) that year and he seems to have developed his grandfather's love for horses. My father loved horses. He combined his love for horses and appreciation for humor by telling the story of a horse he had back in Italy. Joe said he worked hard training the horse not to eat and the horse up and died on him.

When my father came to Rockport I don't think there was another Italian family in town: now I mean Rockport, not Pigeon Cove. There was an Italian enclave in the Cove. The Italians in the Cove came from farther north in Italy, Lombardy, than my father so there was no real connection between them in the old country.

Soon after my father came to Rockport, Henry Barletta came here too. Henry came from my Bonito, my father's home town. I don't think they knew each other in Italy because Henry was ten years or so younger than my father. Henry lived with my mother and father for his first few months in town, probably about 1916. When my mother died in 1975 (many years after my father's death) Henry told me with tears in his eyes how generous and good my parents were to him.

A native Rockporter told my husband Walter that in his childhood there were many Sunday dinners that were owed to Joe Pascucci. If Joe heard that children might be going hungry he had to help where he could. But he wouldn't say say anything about that sort of thing, sometimes not even to my mother. Although my father was emotional, he wasn't all that talkative. He was a quiet man; not that he was incapable of seeing humor here and there, but his note of humor was apt to be quiet.

My brother Anthony graduated from Rockport High School in 1932. He went to the Louisiana State University and did four years of study in three years, stressing pre-med courses. Tony was more bookish than his two brothers, John and Patsy. He applied to medical school but was too late for that year, finding that he had to wait another year before he could enter. He was very dis-

appointed after cramming all that work into such a short time, so he went to Bentley instead and became an accountant, eventually working for Sears, Roebuck.

My brother John was drafted in 1942, and Tony felt badly that his year younger brother was in military service and he wasn't. By then Tony had married and had a little boy but in 1944 Tony joined the Navy. Just a year later he was killed off Okinawa. It was later discovered that if he hadn't volunteered, his draft number would never have come up. Tony could speak Italian beautifully and while in the Navy began to study Russian. John lives in Pigeon Cove and Patsy lives in the Worcester area.

Joe Pascucci worked on Rockport shoes from 1912 to 1951. He had to finally give up his place in his sunny window, dying in 1953, insisting that he be buried in Rockport, the town he loved so much. Toward the end of his life his health deteriorated, in part a result of having lost Anthony in 1945.

My mother had quite a household to care for when I was born: my father, my three teen-age brothers and her own elderly father. There was plenty of housework to be done, so she taught me basic things, like how to dust the furniture, when I was six or seven years old. I helped my mother as much as I could but never felt put upon in this mostly male household. I also helped by ironing the flat things: pillow cases, handkerchiefs, sheets, etc.

My brothers were very good to me: it was as if I had three or four fathers. When I was two years old, my brother Tony was already out of the house. . .there was that much of an age gap. Nearly every morning when I was little I'd run into my brothers' room (being the only girl, I had a room to myself and they had to share) and they treated me so well: teaching me things like simple arithmetic. I have only pleasant memories of my three brothers.

One time my father caught the boys smoking a cigarette. "So," he said, "you boys want to smoke? Come with me." He gave each of them an Italian stogie (a harsh twist of tobacco that is known for its strength) and told them to take a few puffs. All three got sick long before they had finished the stogies.

The three boys had one bicycle to share. My mother told me she could never remember hearing them argue, even over the use of the bicycle. She said they were always laughing. But they were told to use the bicycle only in the driveway: not out in the street. One day my father, on his way home for lunch (he closed his shop from 12 to 1 every day and walked home to High Street), and met one of the boys with the bicycle at the junction of Parker and High Streets (where the plaque in memory of Antonio Pascucci is displayed) with the bicycle. He brought the bicycle home and vigorously dismantled it. That was the end of that one bicycle for three boys. They had done what they were not supposed to do and in those days such a thing called for a punishment that would have some meaning to it. My father, of course, was fearful that they'd get hurt out on the street, and they needed this rather strong reminder that he was not to be disobeyed. My father would assert himself only with a firm "Ahem!" when we were doing something he didn't approve of and when we heard that sound we stopped whatever it was we weren't supposed to be doing. I don't remember his ever spanking us.

The only time I remember hearing about a spanking happened when the boys went over to Stimson's Pond one winter day. Patsy, being perhaps the most adventurous of the three, managed to fall into the icy water and headed home soaking wet, escorted by a gang of boys. My mother took off his clothes, put him in a hot tub, and while she was drying him off gave him a real old-fashioned spanking, saying that he'd better not do anything like that again. I don't think he did!

Louella Nickerson and her mother lived next door to us and I was petrified of them. Both of them were a bit "off" or "different". Louella did all sorts of weird things. There was a driveway between their house and ours, and the Nickersons couldn't seem to understand that it was a common driveway for both places. They made my father's life miserable; he was the only one using the driveway. One day he found them both standing in the middle of the driveway, and they wouldn't get out of the way. He shouted at them to get out of the way but they still didn't move. So he finally just had it and backed the car up and came right at them. They got out of the way just in time. Judge York (a Rockporter) had to clarify and settle the issue of the common driveway. Louella told him that my parents were from a strange country and didn't understand English very well. Judge York told them that it was they who didn't understand, that my mother and father understood everything very well, and it was they who were at fault trying to block the driveway.

My father and mother bought two houses on Forest Street. After work in the evening they'd go over to paint and paper them and generally fix them up for resale. They were always thinking of ways to better themselves. They were not lazy; that was the whole secret to success in those days, the willingness to work.

When my father and mother had three little babies, a kind Rockport woman came into his shop and she brought in some baby shoes that her children had outgrown. She wanted to give them to my father for his children. At first my father thought she wanted something done to them but when he understood what she wanted to do with them he handed the shoes back to her. He told her that he could buy shoes for his own children. The woman didn't know that you couldn't give my father anything he had not earned.

The sculptor, Richard Recchia, came into my father's shop once and asked for something to be done to his shoes and my father couldn't quite understand what he wanted done. Recchia responded that he was high strung and emotional about some things. My father said that if Recchia was nervous so was he and he threw his shoes out the door. Recchia brought them back in with great apologies, calmed down and explained what he wanted more carefully. Richard had a local reputation of being very affectedly "artistic" but that didn't wash with my father.

I find it fascinating that people like my parents, known as "foreigners" in those days, came to this country not knowing the language very well, yet made their way, not expecting anything to be given to them . . . not only just made their way but doing better than that. They supplied a warm home for their family, good food and plenty of it without expecting anything. They worked and they contributed.

My mother always said that the people of Rockport were very good to her and to my father. It was the good Doctor Tupper who came to my father when my father was just a young man, and he said that he was going to sell his Main Street building next to where my father was at the time and that he (Dr. Tupper) would like to see my father buy it. And Mr. Bradley at the bank was very helpful and kind. And last but hardly least was Doctor Cleaves, who took care of my parents and us children. My mother often said that Doctor Cleaves had earned a very special place in heaven.

Harrison Cady's studio on Atlantic Avenue. The structure was moved from the remains of the cotton mill on Broadway after it was destroyed by fire. This building has been expanded quite a bit but can still be spotted opposite the intersection with Clark Avenue.

JOHN KIELINEN

Born in 1912 in Pigeon Cove. I was a neighbor to John for nearly 30 years. I bought the building at 16 Mt. Locust Avenue in which John's brother Matt once housed his plumbing business and over the years made it into a comfortable home and studio. One of my changes was to fill in the swampy back yard and build a fairly extensive vegetable garden. Every once in a while John would show up and quietly stand and watch me as I worked the soil, seldom commenting, but I had the distinct feeling that if he had seen anything seriously amiss in my gardening approaches I would have heard about it.

MY MOTHER AND FATHER were both born in Finland. They came to this country in 1904 or 1905. They came right to Pigeon Cove. I remember the boarding house that was once next door to this house (239 Granite street). My grandfather, father and uncle lived in that boarding house for a while. Before my father married my mother he had worked in iron ore mines, but after coming to Pigeon Cove he worked in the granite quarries. I don't really remember that but I do remember those old lunch pails they carried to work. They were pretty deep and the top half was for hot coffee or tea to drink with their lunch.

When the quarry workers got new hammers they had to test them out before using them at work. You can find a lot of drill holes in granite ledges around here but most of them don't mean anything: they were made by workers testing their hammers. The handle had to just so or it would jar your arm, so they'd wrap a piece of leather around it to take up some of the shock of hammering the drills.

When we were kids the old time quarry workers would sit around and dream a bit: talking about some kind of system much like Social Security today. They really wanted to see something like that in their old age, after spending a lifetime working. Roosevelt came along and put it in for the country, and now we have Medicare and Social Security.

I was born on Curtis Street on March 9, 1912. I've lived my life within this quarter mile area of Pigeon Cove. When I was growing up everybody had hogs and chickens for meat and eggs. The hogs were slaughtered when the cold weather began to set in. The meat was salted down in tubs and barrels for winter keeping. Everyone also kept a vegetable garden for vegetables, which were stored in sand for the winter. Potatoes and apples were also stored over.

Several people kept cows; like Jacob Ranta who lived on Curtis Street: the Rantas were our milk people; they would deliver milk in a big can through a short cut between our houses. They'd bring two big cans and a measuring thing they'd measure out the milk with. There was a lot of milk around in those days because so many people kept cows; mainly for their own family use, but some sold what they didn't need or couldn't use.

The biggest farms were Charlie Balzarini's farm on Curtis Street and Antone Balzarini's farm at the Babson Farm (site of the present day Old Farm Inn at 291 Granite Street). They also had a meat business. They had regular customers who they sold fresh meat to; meat that they had butchered right there on the farm. It was a treat to get a ride on the horse and sleigh in the winter as they delivered milk. Those were the days as kids when we didn't know enough to worry.

Many people were dependent on the quarry work and ran up a grocery bill at the company store in the winter, when they couldn't work the quarries. Then they paid it up as the cash flow began again in the spring and summer. The Finns, Swedes and Italians all had their own communities, and language could have been a barrier at times in the quarries.

The Rockport Granite Company store sold some work clothes and groceries to their workers. Here in Pigeon Cove there were several stores: Story's Market, a store on Pigeon Hill Street and John Martin's store on Stockholm Avenue. There was also a cobbler, Andrew Niemi, a post office and Savinen's bakery here in Pigeon Cove. There were two Finnish markets on Forest Street in Rockport. Those Finn stores would come and take orders on one day and deliver it the next day: they delivered food as well as kerosene for the lamps. At one time there were 5 churches in Pigeon Cove.

My mother went to the Finnish Lutheran church. There were two Lutheran churches around here; one in Lanesville and another on Forest Street in Rockport; they shared the same minister. He had a parsonage in Peabody. Neither my mother or father were joiners but they did have something to do with the Lutheran Sunday schools. All of the church services and Sunday school lessons were given in Finnish.

In the church, when you were fifteen or sixteen years old, you had to go to confirmation school. This was a two week session with the minister. You had to learn by heart certain sections of both the history of the Bible and as it was written in modern times. At that age you were supposed to able to reason things out. You had to learn everything in Confirmation school in Finnish.

My parents used oil lamps at night until they bought their own home. . .it was a big improvement when someone invented a reflector to put behind the wall oil lamp to increase the light source. When our house was wired for electricity we had just the one light hanging from the middle of a ceiling in a room. You could see the wires inside the bulbs and they didn't throw off very much light.

Our house was heated by a large black stove in the kitchen. Over the stove was a hole cut for a register to let heat into the bedrooms upstairs. In the winter that stove was the only heat: there really wasn't that much heat because the fire in the stove burned out every night. Coal was hard to come by in those days, so our stove was heated with wood. All the cooking was done on that stove and it seemed that oatmeal and a tin pot of coffee was always on the stove. Later on we had an oil stove with two or three burners for cooking but there was no heating unit there.

I remember my father coming home after working in the Babson Farm quarry. He always left something in his lunch pail for Matt and me (Matt was John's younger brother). That was hard living because in bad weather they could not work the quarries. I remember my father and other men going to the lumber camp to cut wood. My mother used to pack two suitcases full of clean clothes and non-perishable dried food. After a long time he would come back home.

Before coming into the house they had to unpack outdoors so the cockroaches didn't get into the house. I remember wondering if the roaches and bed bugs had all gone. The stores sold a lot of bug poison in those days. Living in those days was not like it is living today.

When I was a kid we'd go and get blue-berries in the woods and blackberries along the shore. We'd sell the berries to the people who lived on the Avenues. We got 15 or 20 cents a quart for the berries, many of which were preserved for use in the winter. No one questioned anybody about where you could or could not walk along the shore or in the woods back then. But new people came in, bought property and shut people out. They came to this quaint town and then wanted to change it.

We had clamp-on ice skates (to be clamped onto one's shoes) when we were kids and they would loosen the heels on your shoes after you used them a while. When you had ice shoe-skates you really had something! The only ice we had to skate on was two places across the street from here: the Witch House property. We called them Oregon and Silver Lake. If you fell in it was only in about two feet of water. But it made a good place for ice buckling (a process of running fast enough across this ice so you didn't fall in). Most of us had makeshift sleds: only a few kids had Flexible Flyers.

Along Andrew's Point and Halibut Point was good fishing when the cunners came in along the rocks. You could get a good mess of cunners there almost any time. The best time was in the summers and fall. We used to go fishing two or three times a week. In the fall the tautogs came in (a larg-er, cunner-like fish). The best place for tau-togs was Halibut Point. Once I got eighteen in three days.

One time when I went along that path to Halibut Point the entire area was covered with snakes sunning on the rocks. Every time after that I checked to see if there any snakes around. Beautiful wild roses grew all along that shore path to Halibut Point. We used crabs caught from tide pools for tautog bait. At one time we would go to the Pigeon Cove harbor for the little green crabs but when the Tool Company went to oil for their power and heat the tankers spilled oil into the harbor and ruined that source of bait.

Most Finnish kids my age learned how to talk, read and write Finnish. Almost every Finn home had at least two Finn newspapers. The papers came every day: they came from the Fitchburg and New York areas. One paper had to do with church activities and the other dealt with more current events. One paper was called the Raivaja (The Pioneer) and the other, the Communist one, was called the Forward. I didn't belong to the Temperance Society but I borrowed books from their library and read about such knowledge. When or wherever a Finn Hall was established, the first thing they would put in would be a library. I now subscribe to a Finnish newspaper that comes once a week.

When my brother Matt and I went to school we couldn't talk English. We only spoke Finnish. Whatever our cultural back-ground was, we went to school to learn English. As kids, we may have had some gripes but my parents said that the teachers were right and to do as the teachers say. Some of my friends wanted to have school and others didn't. I would have liked to have had more schooling. Matt built a successful plumbing businesss. He was one of the youngest Master plumbers in the state. He had plans that he wanted to do but he died too young to see his dreams. Matt died at the age of 50 of a heart attack.

Matt and his wife Rachel (sister of John's wife Sylvia; their maiden name was Jacobson: two brothers married two sisters) were the ones who developed Boulder Top, with that great view of Sandy Bay and Rockport.* Look at all the tax dollars up there now . . . all those big condominiums they have built up there. Matt and Rachel had a motel business up there and Matt had always planned to someday spend his summers in Rockport and his winters in Florida. He never saw that. Rachel ran the central motel with about six units after Matt died, and some cottages besides that, but when she reached retirement age she sold off each unit separately. Matt and Rachel did that whole thing the hard way.

We had what were called the church Finns and the Hall Finns. The Hall Finns were either at Temperance Hall on Forest Street or the Socialist Hall on Squam Hill (*present site of Tuck's candy factory*). We liked the Socialist Hall because they had the best dance floor there. It was never a Communist Hall; they were Socialists. The Socialists have mellowed and some of them are like Republicans now.

I didn't know it as a kid but the church Finns and the Hall Finns didn't get along. But they finally learned to work together as one community. During the Winter War and World War II all Finns united and sent packages over to Finland.

We had a Finnish Athletic Club at the Squam Hill Hall, and we'd have marching drills and build human pyramids, stuff like that. I was always on the bottom. Andrew Niemi was the leader: he used to have athletic classes over there and we had a lot of fun with him.

We also had a basketball team, with the Silva brothers, Snap and Jim, Dyke Brown, Flemmy Flanders, Bruno Pearson, Tom Dolan . . . a lot of local guys. We were pretty good when we played in our own league but when we played away from home we weren't all that good. The Athletic Club sponsored several track meets at Evans Field. I was more into track and field than basketball, but I became manager of the basketball team and made arrangements for our games.

Before my time a man by the name of Woolford (*OddieBoy*) had a stable on the water side of Phillips Avenue, opposite Lindley Dean's brick house. Near the water was an underground tunnel to take the horses back to the stable. OddieBoy and Charlie Balestraci used to race horses along Phillips Avenue. Charlie told me that the winning horse got a bag of oats. They usually had races about Thanksgiving time.

Along by Cathedral Rocks (*across the street from the Ralph Waldo Emerson hotel*) there used to be three tennis courts for the summer people. They'd play either tennis or lawn croquet. In the old days there was a tennis court just to the left of Reed's Lane, where Mrs. Lindley Dean built her last house. Right below the Denghausen's (*31 Phillips Avenue, now owned by William James*) there was a swimming hole in the rocks.

*Matt was at one time captain of the author's volunteer fire company and I remember him describing how he managed to get precious building materials during World War II and right after it. He said he'd dress himself up in a clean pair of overalls and a chambray work shirt buttoned up to the chin but with no necktie. He found out where to go to apply for these scarce materials and he'd stand out in the center of the large entrance space gawking around with his hat in his hand until one of the bureaucrats took pity on him and asked if they could help him . . . and they were doomed. Matt always went home with permission to obtain what he needed.

They built a bulkhead to hold the water in when the tide went out and they had heavy ropes strung along the rocks for bathers to hang on when the waves came in.

There used to be a beautiful stone building called Way Villa right there on Andrew's Point, but they tore it down for some reason. It was the best building on the Point in its time. I used to deliver papers there, and it was a long hike to get there from the foot of Powsel's Hill, where the papers were dropped off. But I got a good tip.

Further along Andrew's Point the Atlantic Path came to Andrew's Hollow: sometimes labelled Hoop Pole Cove on some maps. In that cove was an area about 35,000 square feet that was and is still owned by the Town. When we were much younger four or five couples of us used to have picnics there by the shore and enjoy ourselves. As a matter of fact, we saw the Russian Sputnik go overhead from that spot. Right above the little gravel "beach" in the cove is an old granite foundation of what used to be a horse barn, at the end of Long Branch Avenue. At one time the owners of the hotels and boarding houses in the area got together and cleared the rocks from Hoop Pole Cove and made it one of the best little bathing beaches on the Cape. We played there as children, as did my daughters and nieces after us.

Pigeon Cove, particularly the Andrew's Point area, was a summer resort long before Rockport got into the act. There were a lot of hotels and rooming houses here. They were not the type of tourists we see today; they stayed for longer periods of time along the Avenues section of the Cove. Whenever we heard the fire alarm for the Avenues area sound off we'd say, "There's another hotel burning." Most of them burned down but there were never any people in them when that happened. All but the Ocean View House burned down. That house and the annex across LaCross Avenue were torn down piece by piece. Mrs. Lindley Dean bought the property.

There used to be three fish outfits in Pigeon Cove harbor. One where the Pigeon Cove Fishermen's Co-op is now, one at the parking lot and another on what eventually became the Tool Company steel storage yard along Breakwater Avenue. They'd land fish at these places and ice them down to be put in the big trucks that came to haul them away. Some Pigeon Cove fish made their way to the Fulton Fish Market in New York City.

At one time the former Lindley Dean house at 27 Phillips Avenue (now owned by the Printys) was a wooden house with shingled siding and was called the New Okdene House. It looks like a brick house now, but there's a wooden house inside it. My father took care of the furnaces in this place and Jud Dean's house next door, up Ocean Avenue: this later became the Caffrey house. My father was given the chance to buy the Caffrey house but he didn't have enough money to do so.

When we were growing up my father wanted to buy some land in this area (*the area roughly bordered by Granite Street, Phillips Avenue, Haven and Ocean Avenues*). But the agent at that time, a man named Shackelford, wouldn't sell it to him because he said that we (being Finns) didn't have enough money to build a house big or good enough for the area. After he either died or moved on, a local real estate agent, Helen Thurston, took a mortgage on the properties in the neighborhood which allowed my father to finally buy it. The land included this house where I have spent the past 58 years with my wife and family.

My parents owned much of the land between Haven Avenue and Phillips Avenue. There was a boarding house next door and Ivar Wiik owned the rest of the land. My mother gave me and my brother Matt each a lot after my father died, and we built our houses on them. My sister Laila lived in the small house in back of this one for a while.

My father died on December 1, 1927 and I had to go to work on the 19th of that month. I was only fifteen years old. I wanted to stay in school, I had only a year and a half of high school, but I had to quit. It was a question of whether you wanted to stop eating or whether you wanted to go to school. In those day there were no places where you could get help or aid. Most of the Finns wouldn't have wanted to accept any help either.

After my father died, my mother took in washing. She'd wash and iron them and us kids would deliver them. I was trying to go to school and after school I had a job as a floor sweeper in the machine shop of the Cape Ann Tool Company. I think I got the job as much for sympathy as for anything else, for my father's tending the furnaces in the Dean houses. I was really too young to start to work, but I'd work in the afternoons after school and on Saturdays. The Company used to work all day Saturday in those days.

We made a lot of stuff at the Tool Company. When I first went in there it was mostly for Mack trucks and the Autocar Company making heavy equipment like that. Our drop forgings here were then sent off to a machine shop for finishing. I had to be eighteen before I could work on a machine. One time I was working on a drill

press and ripped my hand open and had to have eighteen stitches: I was holding a big die up and there was blood all over the floor. While working on a lathe one time a steel chip flew and cut the cornea of my right eye. I only saw shadows out that eye until 1992, when an eye doctor sent me to Boston for testing and later, for five operations. Because of modern medical advances I was able to see out of that eye for the first time in over 50 years! However, I had still been able to hold down a job at the Tool Company while only seeing well out of one eye. I've worked at the Company ever since those after school days and worked at everything but drop forging. I wound up being a die sinker.

During the Great Depression I managed to get five weeks work out of the CWA (*the Civilian Works Administration*). They had the CCC (*Civilian Conservation Corps*) at the same time. They built those camps, and did a lot of good work. The Finns didn't want to go into that stuff. They hated anything with a uniform because they had been under Swedish and Russian rule for so many years and a uniform signified repression.

In the early days Finland was a backward country; they had no education of any kind way back. Under Swedish rule the Swedes would send the ministers over there to preach and they'd preach in Swedish, and the Finns didn't understand that. The Finns didn't have much to do with religion in the old days: way back the Finns had one saint: I think it was Saint Henry. In the winter time all the Finnish lakes were frozen over and they didn't take much to Henry and put an axe to his back and murdered him and then made a saint out of him.

One day in 1938 John Francis and George Story said I should take out papers for cemetery commissioner. I did and I got elected. I think I was the first one to complete a three year term. Beech Grove cemetery had a lot of problems that we got cleared up: some of those lots sold for seven dollars and fifty cents. We got the cemeteries all mapped out and established a new set of rules.

I also served on the Board of Health during the war. I was appointed and members of the Board said they'd resign if I accepted. I told the Selectmen that they could withdraw my appointment, but they said they wouldn't: there needed to be a change on the Board. I asked one of the protesters what he had against me he said he didn't know me and I told him it wouldn't take long to get to know me. Another member said I wasn't wanted on the Board because I couldn't take shorthand, but neither could he. I think the real reason was that my brother Matt refused to hook up someones sewer to a catch basin and they tried to get back at Matt by saying I wasn't wanted on the Board. But I got on.

During my time we started the first real effort to sewer the town with the aid of State and Federal monies. Our beaches used to be very polluted and our warning signs were torn down. We appointed Sterling Poole* as the town sanitary inspector. He had a degree from MIT and we thought he was very qualified.

We also hired Jack Lawler** as the first town garbage collector. Jack had taken courses at Harvard but he had to go to work to help support his family. He served as town garbage collector for a good many years. I also served on a study committee for building codes and a committee for a new high school.

I'm proud to have served on these town boards. I've had a good life living and growing up in Rockport.: with my wife of 58 years, Sylvia, and my two wonderful daughters. I'm proud to be a native Rockporter and proud of my Finnish heritage.

---

*As with many locals, Mr. Poole soon acquired a nickname: one of the more apt nicknames in Rockport history: "Cess" Poole.

** Jack Lawler was a well known sight around town for many years as he made pertinent comments on almost any subject while collecting garbage: known all over Rockport for his back-of-the-truck soliloquies.

The Gott house on Gott Avenue in the Halibut Point area of Pigeon Cove. This is a very rare half gambrel house; the oldest standing gambrel roofed house on Cape Ann. Built in 1702.

MIRIAM NIEMI LANE

*Born in Lanesville on Norseman Avenue in
1919. Her sister Meri was also born in
Lanesville. Both girls were marvelously talented
musicians and Miriam is the possessor of one of
the finer senses of humor on Cape Ann. I have
never conversed with her for more than a few
minutes before both of us enjoy a good laugh.
She is a joy to be around. Miriam is Mrs.
Charles Lane, and has been for 46 years;
Charles Lane of Lane's Farm on South Street.
My wife usually meets her Thursdays at the
IGA as Miriam stocks up on cat food for the
farm barn cats.*

M
Y MAIDEN NAME NIEMI is a shortened version of the original name.
That name was Syrjaniemi before it became
Americanized. Both of my parents came
from Finland: they met over here. My mother came from a Swedish speaking part of
Finland. Her maiden name was Sulin, which
was Swedish. My father Andrew ran away
from home when he was quite young to join
the circus, eventually making his way to this
country. My father worked in the granite
quarries. But he didn't like that and started
his own shop in Pigeon Cove and did shoe
repairing. He had a sign made in the shape
of a shoe and on it said "Niemi Shoe
Hospital."

My father was a comedian of sorts.
While he'd be tapping on shoes he'd be making up words. His store sold a lot of things
besides shoe repairing: clothes for the Tool
Company, he even sold those big Victrolas
(early wind-up record playing machines). He
started his Pigeon Cove store while we still
lived in Lanesville; he took his bicycle to the
Cove every morning in those days.

We moved from Lanesville to Pigeon

Cove when I was ten years old. We lived
beside the Pigeon Cove chapel. It was a
wonderful place, the land went right down
to the ocean. We went swimming every
morning before breakfast. We lived in that
house for two or three years and then we
moved to Pigeon Hill Street.

I went to the school opposite Peter
Bernard's Garage (now Burbank Auto at 66
Granite Street) set back from the road down
toward the water. In the Lane School in
Lanesville when we learned to read and
write we had to hold the pen a certain way
*(from her description of finger positioning I
assume it to have been the Palmer Method)* The
minute we began to write in Pigeon Cove we
could write it any old way. When they first
built the Story School on Story Street in
Pigeon Cove I was in one of the first grades
to use it.

My father had an older brother who also
came to this country. He was a great speaker
and went around lecturing in both Finnish
and English. He had a great speaking voice
and lectured at colleges and universities. He
was an editor of Finnish newspapers in this
country. He was an editor in Ohio and the
Pacific Northwest; Washington and Oregon,
where he also edited. He came back to New
York and edited a Brooklyn Finnish paper.

There were a lot of Finnish Communists
on Cape Ann in the old days, especially in
Lanesville and Pigeon Cove. After we
bought the Story store in Pigeon Cove in
the forties a man walked into the store one
day and said he was from the F.B.I. He asked
if any of us knew anybody who was a
Communist. He stationed himself in the
Pigeon Cove Post Office and watched for
who got the Finnish Communist newspaper.

It was called the Forward in English.

I began piano lessons when I was seven years old. My sister and I took music lessons all along the way and switched to Hannah Grover in Rockport when we moved to Pigeon Cove. When I was about eleven years old we started the accordion. There were two women accordion players along with a man who played the violin (three Finns) who made numerous trips around the country to various Finnish Halls. They'd play a concert for about an hour and then play for dancing for three hours. After one Cape Ann concert my parents had them come to our house for dinner and my mother ordered an accordion from one of the women accordionists, Viola Turpeinen. It was made in Italy and was all gold; it was beautiful and had my sister's name (Meri) on it in red.

My father told stories,* wrote songs and also played a horn in the Lanesville Waino band. He was an exceptional athlete. The local Finns were great gymnasts, even the girls were acrobatic. We met in the old Universalist Church on the lower corner of Phillips Avenue and Granite Street after it was through being used as a church. The church is gone and all that's left now is a small empty lot. We met there three nights a week. We had tumbling mats and practised various exercises, like making pyramids. We were always on the bottom and Allie Enos was on top because she was small. It was a blast to do that.

Young men like Pingree Hillier and Charlie Nelson and Jorma Savinen did many different physical gymnastic tricks. We'd all put on exhibitions from time to time. The girls all wore white blouses and

middy bloomers for the performances. My father put on one performance in the Town Hall. When we were going to high school we built high jumps and things like that in our back yard so we could do our calisthenics after school, broad jumping, shot puts, and stuff like that.

When we were still kids my sister and I began playing our accordions for different local events and places. When Franklin Roosevelt was running for President (either the first or second time) we were still kids but were asked to play at a political rally in the Gloucester City Hall. There were a few Roosevelts present: James, Elliot and Franklin Jr., who was married to the beautiful Ethel DuPont (she was there) all sitting on the City Hall stage. We were right in the front row, ready to get up and play when needed. We played between speeches. We also did a lot of minstrel shows. They were popular back then. We had covered a lot of Finnish Halls all over New England by this time, staying overnight with Finnish families. We'd entertain with my father singing his songs for about an hour and then we'd play for dancing afterward.

My father had been entertaining all around New England by this time and we traveled with him to accompany him. The year I should have graduated from high school was the year we went to New York. My father got the call to come to New York and make some Victor Records of his songs (in Finnish of course.) We were doing a lot of touring at the time anyway, and sometimes we'd get back from an engagement so tired that we couldn't get up in the morning and would miss school that way. The school superintendent had told us before that we

---

*Andrew Niemi became known as a Finnish standup comic as well as an all around entertainer.

either had to quit touring or quit school. I was that close, just a month away from graduation when we got the call to go to New York. We had to go to New York at that time because my father's agent had it all set up. I've always regretted not graduating. My father wanted Meri to accompany him on the piano for the recordings but she had jammed her fingers in a sliding door in school. He took her anyway but she wasn't needed because they had a studio band standing by to back him up and they were terrific.

We appeared with a lot of big show business people during those times: Rudy Vallee, Shep Fields, Vincent Price, people like that. When we played in Greenwich Village we met Phil Baker (*a big name in his day*) and he invited us to attend his Sunday radio broadcast from a New York theater. We wore our long gowns and he seated us in the balcony practically overlooking the stage. We looked out at the audience and they were all looking up at us, probably thinking we were important people.

We played the Winter Garden and met Ozzie and Harriet. We played all over, from Alabama to upstate New York, where we performed with Gracie Fields. One time we met Jimmy Durante, Martha Ray and Eddie Duchin and got to sit down with them. Walter Winchell even mentioned us in his newspaper column, wondering who those two blond accordion players were.

I met all my father's people when we went over to Finland. My sister and I went over when I was sixteen; we played the accordion and gave concerts all over Finland. We were there for three months. During the first half of that time we stayed with my mother's relatives and the second half with my father's. Once we gave a concert on a small island that had all Swedish Finn people; they all spoke Swedish and we didn't understand a word they said.

I met Paavo Nurmi* in Finland. My sister and I played all over the country. My uncle (my mother's brother) had it all planned ahead of time. We played on the boat going over, too. But we paid our way; it wasn't for the fare. People being how they are, when they heard we were performers said to go ahead and perform, so we did. We played in all three classes of passengers: first class, second class and tourist. We sat with an actor from England and I danced with him: I was only 16. We wore long gowns when we performed so we were all set for dancing.

My father's people in the northern part of Finland were so religious they wouldn't come to hear us. We stayed with them for a week but they didn't believe in movies, dancing, theaters, nothing. We took the train everywhere we went: my uncle had set it all up but he didn't come with us. We had always used Finnish at home so we had no language difficulty. As a matter of fact, after our tour was completed we played in a night club in Helsinki. In the club we had a band backup and the piano player liked my sister and he knew Paavo. He became a major composer in Finland. I've had correspondence with him: I had to tell him my sister died (she died when she was only 45). He went with my sister and I went with a saxophone player and they took us to another club to eat and that's where we met Paavo Nurmi.

One time when JFK was running for

*Paavo Nurmi: a world famous Finnish marathon runner. He was called "The Flying Finn."

65

Mismatch

Senator he appeared at the Gloucester House restaurant. Ben Smith, a Gloucester boy who was a Harvard room mate of Kennedy's, got us to play for the campaign visit. They had chairs set up outside in the open air and we wore sailor hats and played a lot of sea chanteys and songs like that. Jack and Jackie walked through the crowd, and came right over to sit down next to us. We played, they spoke, and after they made their speeches we played again. And they both came right over to us again and shook our hands. Ben told us that on the way back to Boston in the car the Kennedys asked, "Who were those musicians?"

We broadcast on Sunday mornings on radio station WAAB with a Polish orchestra. Then we got our own little radio show on WHDH and our theme song was "Sophisticated Lady".

In 1943 the Story family asked us if we would like to buy their store.* We bought it and never went back to show business. We had to stay home and run that stupid store. My sister and mother and I ran the place and we lived upstairs above it. We sold the store to the Arujo's from Gloucester after running it for about ten years and then we moved across the street into my father's shop building and lived there. We made it into a restaurant. That was in what is now the old Tool Company parking lot. At one time there was Parson's Drug Store in that same block as my father's store. I still have the chandelier from that Drug Store up in the attic. He had a beautiful fountain with stools and a place in back where you could sit in booths to eat your ice cream and banana splits.

Even with all that, we were still performing around the area at night. When we performed around here we wore gypsy costumes. We wore those great big gold rings on shower curtains for earrings, with elastic holding them on our heads. I've played with quite a few local musical groups, like Del Mitchell and Billy Crowell. I still play piano at Spiran Hall, and accordion with the Cape Ann Finnish Singers, the Birka Lodge in Hamilton and the children's Swedish Dancers.

I also played music for the Finnish Dancers of Cape Ann. We played all around New England and one time performed at Constitution Hall in Washington, D. C. I accompanied the Cape Ann Finnish Singers and we performed at a Suomi College Finnfest in Michigan. Betty Graham and Allie Enos were also very important to both these groups. We were and are very proud of our heritage.

*The Story store was across Granite Street from Andrew Niemi's shoe store. That address still has the long, steep flight of steps leading to the front door but is now a private residence.

The "Witch House" at 188 Granite Street in Pigeon Cove. It was built by two young men for their mother, who had been accused of witchcraft in Salem Village (now Danvers). Built in 1692.

ROGER H. MARTIN

Born in the Addison Gilbert Hospital in Gloucester in September, 1925. Except for eleven years off Cape (World War II and postwar) Martin has lived his entire life in Rockport: former deputy Forest Warden, 20+ years in the Rockport Fire Department, elected twice to the Planning Board, served on the Board of Appeals, Rockport's first Poet Laureate, founding faculty member, professor emeritus and honorary doctor of fine arts of what is now the Montserrat College of Art in Beverly, Mass. Author of "Rockport Remembered" and "A Rockport Album" also published by the Curious Traveller Press.

I SUBMIT THIS "INTERVIEW" with myself with more than a little trepidation but feel qualified to include myself in a group of people who belong to a second immigrant generation of Rockporters. Even though my father's Azorean forebears became Americans some generations ago, my mother came from Finland in 1904 at the age of seven, in steerage wth her mother and two siblings. Such a marriage of Nordic and Iberian backgrounds are not all that unusual on Cape Ann: the Portuguese having come for the fishing and many Scandanavians to the granite quarrying industry. Nowadays the fishing has become almost a marginal occupation because of stringent restrictions intended to restore the fish stocks and the granite industry per se has long since closed down, due in the main to the introduction of steel and poured concrete as prime building materials.

The actual history of how my Portuguese ancestors came to America has been lost through a family-wide failure to record any of our previous history. My father,

who was known as a talented and creative truth-stretcher, said that we don't even know for sure if our name is really Martin. He thought it might be either Enos, Martinez or Annunzio. One family legend had our ancestor as a member of a Portuguese crew on a full rigged sailing vessel. The crew supposedly mutinied and killed the English captain whose name was Martin. Our ancestor, the story continued, was the only crew member who knew navigation and he was elected captain, taking the captain's name to hide the mutiny. Quite robustly romantic but totally unverifable.

The only surviving log of the Martin sea-going clan is the report from the Rockport Review that has been preserved under glass and is hanging next to my computer along with the flag from the fishing boat Nellie Florence, out of Rockport. The following is an exact quote from this print out.

"Flag of the Nellie Florence and Account from Rockport Review of December, 1886 of her Loss———-

The crew of one of our small boats, Nellie Florence which we mentioned in our last week's issue, returned home safely to their friends, who had been watching so anxiously for them, on the four o'clock train, Monday afternoon. They relate the following story:

After slipping their cable back of Salvages, Thursday they beat until about 7 o'clock, but were obliged to put out their only remaining anchor as a drag that soon parted. They then used a hogshead tub for the same purpose for 36 hours. The seas continually washed across the deck and the cold added to their sufferings. Their water cask was washed overboard, and what little food they had they were unable to reach as it was below the hatches and they feared they would be swamped if they removed them. They ate raw potatoes and molasses from Thursday until the following Sunday. They hoisted their flag union down to attract the attention of some passing sail; once a brig hove to but shortly after went her way, as did a schooner which they afterward signalled. The wind changed Sunday morning to east, enabling them to run for land making Cape Elizabeth at 12 o'clock Sunday noon; not being able to weather it they run into Old Orchard where they were kindly cared for by Mr. and Mrs. T. B. Hough and Mr. and Mrs. Goodwin and selectman S. G. Dorman who obtained for them their passage home.

The vessel will probably be a total loss. She is owned by Chas. Hodgkins, S. N. Tarr, W. A. Dennis and James Fernald, and valued at $600. No insurance.

The undersigned wish to express their heartfelt thanks to Mr. and Mrs. T. B. Hough, Mr. and Mrs. Goodwin also Selectman S. G. Dorman for their kindness to them while in distresss, Sunday Dec. 5th at Old Orchard Beach.

CAPT. JOSEPH MARTIN
G.W.SAWYER
JAMES BURKE
JOS. MARTIN JR.
Rockport, Dec. 11, 1886"

I never note any boat putting out to sea without recalling this incredible memento of what it was like to put to sea in the days of sail. Captain Joseph Martin was my great grandfather and Joseph Martin Jr. was my grandfather. My father used to tell of an argument he had with his father. His father said that if my father didn't admit that he was wrong he'd find the door at 8 Smith Street, the house of his birth, locked upon his return. My father returned and the door was locked. Being just around the corner from Back Beach he said he scoured the beach, found an abandoned dory, reconditioned it, went to sea and never looked back: another lovely romanticized bit of family history. Joseph Martin Jr. suffered from what was diagnosed as consumption (a medical euphemism for a lot of lung diseases in those days) and one day in 1918 went out into the back yard of 8 Smith Street and shot himself.

I do think my father's determination to show the world something went back to a seventh grade school corridor where he was confronted by the school principal on some matter of school discipline. The principal dismissed him with the comment that he was a Portuguese and wouldn't amount to anything anyway. My father quit school on the spot and it was more than likely then that he decided to go to sea.

He eventually became a master mariner and docking master for the Boston Towboat Company, making tows all up and down the Atlantic Coast as well as Boston harbor dockings and undockings. In his later years after he came ashore he became Pilot Commissioner for the waters from Salem to Newburyport. In that capacity he kept his sea legs by piloting tankers into the Salem power plant and assigning other pilots to their chores. It was his chosen berth to see personally to the docking of these tankers and on one blizzardy night in 1961 he talked his pilot boat skipper, Phil Cahill of Marblehead, into taking him out to the tanker, American Eagle, lying off Baker's Island. Phil tried to talk him into staying ashore on such a miserable night but my father insisted. So out they went.

They fetched up alongside the tanker's rusty hull, coming up to a poorly lit Jacob's ladder in the swirling snow. My father jumped from the rail of Phil's boat to the ladder and Phil let his boat fall away from the tanker on a passing swell. He looked astern and saw that my father had slipped off the ladder. Phil said he saw my father bobbing in the seas, looking up to the deck watch and his last heard words on this earth were, "Throw me a Goddamn line!" The deckhands lit the area and threw my father his requested line which he wrapped around an arm but by then the frigid water had penetrated his greatcoat and stopped his heart. They managed to get him back on board and worked over him but to no avail. I was notified by the Rockport police to meet the tanker the next morning at the Salem dock for identification purposes: my stepmother unable to perform that awful task. As I made my way through the tanker passageways I nearly stumbled upon a ship's gray blanket shrouding an all too familiar silhouette. I joined the captain in his cabin, and had a couple of good solid jolts of whiskey with him as he described all they went through in an attempt to revive my father. My stepmother and I felt that the ladder had been defective and were not surprised to hear that it had been "lost" between Salem and New York on the American Eagle's return voyage.

If he was able to request an engraved epitaph to his life I can't help but think he'd be pleased to know that it might be a repeat of his last words as he hurled them out into the tempest of that February, 1961 night in weather so similar to what his father and grandfather had experienced so long ago in the Nellie Florence.

All three Martins before me became sea captains but I obtained my own captaincy while firmly planted ashore when my fellow members of Speedwell Engine Company 2 in Pigeon Cove elected me their company captain, an honor at which I still marvel.

My mother's history differs from my father's in that she left her native Finland (*the town of Ekenas on the coast*) in 1905 when she was only seven years old, and crossed the ocean in steerage with her mother and two siblings. They came through Ellis Island and my grandmother (who spoke Swedish and Finnish but had no English) managed to get her brood on the wrong train. They were supposedly headed to Titusville, Pennsylvania where, for forgotten reasons, my tailor grandfather had settled when he came to this country before bringing his family over. Such a preliminary male reconnoiter was not unusual in those days. They traveled nearly 200 miles in the wrong direction before a conductor could find someone who spoke Finnish and got them back on the right track. This terribly upsetting experience had long-lasting ramifications. My mother said that it was years before my grandmother would open her door to anyone who couldn't speak Finnish. My grandparents, Arthur F. and Ida E. Oker, lived upstairs from us at 109 Main Street, a place owned by my father. I expect they moved to Rockport from Pennsylvania at the behest of some of their local Finnish friends who suggested that my grandfather might have a more productive business serving Rockports large Scandanavian population.

For most of their lives my mother and grandmother spoke Swedish around the house: they had come from a Swedish speaking section of Finland. One of the many regrets I have in my old age is the mistake of not having been interested in really learning the language. But I did get to understand what they were saying after a while. They were in the habit of speaking Swedish in front of me especially when they didn't want me to know what they were saying. I didn't let on that I could fathom what they were saying for some time and became privy to some family matters about which I perhaps shouldn't have heard. My mother lost any trace of a Swedish accent after being in this country a while but still moved her mouth as she sounded out the English words to herself when she wrote down things like her grocery lists. I loved to pretend to write long before I could form letters of any kind, scribbling pencil marks on stray bits of paper, but all the time moving my mouth as my mother did. I supposed that to be an integral part of the writing process.

On one never to be forgotten Saturday in May, 1932 my grandfather failed to return home for lunch, which he had done without fail for all the 25 years he ran his tailor and haberdashery store on Rockport's Main Street. My grandmother sent her son, my uncle Rudolph, down to the shop to see what had happened. He found all the shades drawn and the door locked. He had to walk all the way back up the hill to the house for the keys and back down and found, to his horror, his father lying on the floor in a pool of blood, having been savagely beaten. He died on the way to the hospital in Gloucester.

I was only seven years old at the time of the murder and have not many concrete memories of that terrible time in our house. All I truly recall is going upstairs to my

grandmother's kitchen, knowing that something was not right in the house, and finding my mother and grandmother holding each other crying their eyes out. I was told to go back downstairs. A rather typical Finnish response (at least in our house) to emotions of any kind. All I knew then was that I had seen the last of my grandfather, the man who held me in his lap, gave me bristley kisses and invariably produced a lollipop from somewhere in his chair cushions.

The seemingly senseless murder stunned the town. Oker had been a respected member of the Swedish Congregational church in Pigeon Cove and had extended credit to practically anyone who asked for it in those Depression days. The police could not imagine a motive for such a brutal assault. The ensuing investigation produced no usable evidence against any of the many suspects interviewed.

This story has a further, even more frightening development. Needless to say, my grandfather's murder had changed an entire way of life in Rockport. The town had formerly been a community of trust and honesty among it's entire citizenry and doors were never locked. But after this murder things changed. Neighbors looked at one another and couldn't help but be nervous and doors were now locked tight and shades drawn at night.

Then, on Halloween night, 1933, the Swedish Congregational church hosted a Halloween party at which Mrs. Augusta Johnson, reportedly a bit in her cups, announced that she knew who murdered Mr. Oker and if that person didn't come forward she would go to the police the next day. Early the next morning smoke was seen coming from an upstairs window in the Johnson house. When the fire department got there they found the house splattered with blood and gore, evidence that Mrs. Johnson had tried in vain to save herself from her attacker by fleeing. She was found naked, bathed in her own blood, tied to her bed and the bed set on fire . . . the work of a madman.

It didn't take a Sherlock Holmes or Perry Mason to figure out that whoever committed both murders still lived in town and was known to all. Needless to say this caused terrible pressures within the community as everyone scrambled to establish alibis for the night of this second murder. There are still people in town who will not speak about those days when a large number of State Troopers were barracked in the Town Hall and went through every house in town searching for clues and finding none. They left town in the middle of November without coming close to solving the murders.

My daughter Rachel has long been interested in this case and prevailed upon me to see what I might find out under the freedom of information law. With this in mind I had occasion to speak with a retired State police officer and asked him if it was true, as put forward by many TV shows, that law officers know full well who has committed a crime but are sometimes unable to put forward a case that could be won in court. He said it happened all too frequently. After he heard about these murders he gave me the name and number of the officer in charge of all State Police records.

I called him up and told him of my grandfather's murder and he was just barely able to hide his boredom at such a question about an event that happened so many years before. But when I told him of the followup Johnson murder I sensed an increase in his attention. I requested access to the State

Police records of their investigation and he laughed as he told me that I'd be appalled at how some of these records were being kept stored in cardboard boxes in hallways of abandoned State Hospitals, but said he'd give it a shot and would call me if he found anything. I thought to myself, sure, sure, and that I'd never hear anything from him. About a week or so later the Lieutenant called me and said that he'd found my grandfathers record box. And it was empty! Talk about wheels within wheels and mysteries within mysteries! So, even this far beyond those horrible events the mystery, instead of being resolved, continues to produce more mysterious goings on. It is physically possible that the perpetrator of these ghoulish murders is still alive and some people in town do believe that to be so. But I'm afraid my daughter is doomed to disappointment when it comes to finding out any more than this about her great-grandfathers murder.

All this mayhem notwithstanding, my life has so far been free of any such bloody events. I enlisted in the U. S. Coast Guard in World War II and served from 1942 to 1946. Following this service I attended the School of the Boston Museum of Fine Arts under the G.I. Bill of Rights. Following graduation I was a free-lance illustrator and graphic designer in Boston and New York for a short time before returning to my roots in 1953 and have lived very contentedly here ever since. It wasn't until I had returned to Rockport that my life began to take on new meaning and offered me the chance to try many different areas of activities in the arts. After selling a continuing series of drawings to the New Yorker magazine and the New York Times, my most enjoyable and most profitable illustration account (for the

View from Main Street to Poole's Drug Store on the corner of Beach and Main Streets and down the street toward Dock Square after an average snowfall.

United Church of Christ) surfaced shortly after my return, followed by a stint as pipe organ pipe shade carver for Charles Fisk and my subsequent 20 year membership on the founding faculty of what has become the Montserrat College of Art in Beverly. And now, this former high school student who carried three English courses in his senior year has had a minor career of sorts as a writer; ten years of regular columns in the Gloucester Daily Times and this third book based upon my home town. My first wife Joan Fertig and I produced three children and were married for 35 years before she succumbed to cancer. I've had the unbelieveably good fortune to have met, fallen in love with, and married Ann Nichols O'Grady and built a whole new life in the Land's End section of Rockport. Only in America. Only in Rockport.

HENRY E. "PAT" HENDRICKSON

Born in 1919, in the Haskins hospital atop Poole's Hill (Summit Avenue) during the flu epidemic, his mother being ill with the flu at his birth. I asked Pat how come he got the nickname Pat and he said it was because his father used to fool around and call him Patrick Henry Hendrickson. Pat and his wife Norma (Shute) are two exemplars of a certain kind of quiet day to day heroism that more often than not remains undetected beneath small town surface pleasantries. Suffice to say that they have undergone more than their share of tragic circumstances yet still retain a sense of proportion and humor about life. They have my utmost respect. I've left this introduction as I originally wrote it but must sadly add the fact that Pat Hendrickson died not all that long after completing our last interview.

MY FATHER WAS BORN in Lansing, Michigan. My mother came from Finland. Her maiden name was Johnson. My father was a Swede but he could talk Finn better than any Finn I ever heard. The Hendrick part of our name was Swedish for Henry.* My father worked with the stone cutters on Finn Alley *(Forest Street)*. He taught me a lot of the Finnish language. You might say I spoke it some, but reluctantly. We went to Sunday school at Saint Paul's Lutheran church right there on Forest Street. Old John Somppi and Matt Toppan tried to teach us the gospel and Christ's life, but that was all in Finnish. So you'd sit there

and you might have understood it in English but in Finnish you didn't get anything but a bunch of sounds.

I grew up during the Depression years. There was very little work for anyone during those years, but my father and grandfather worked in the quarries whenever possible. My mother worked doing housework for the "Yankees", as my older sister called them: people who had money enough to hire household help. My grandmother had to take care of us kids daily while my mother worked. I had three sisters, one who died at around 12 years old.

We had oil lamps, and an oil stove with a portable oven for our cooking and baking. We had outside toilets, an outhouse, which smelled to high heaven. It was cleaned out twice a year by the Balzarini "honey wagon." It was bitter cold to go out there in the winter. We dreaded going out at night. For all practical purposes we were allowed to use a chamber pot during the worst weather. We were given the luxury of an inside toilet when we moved to 11 Forest Street from our house at 2 Forest Street. We moved there to take care of my elderly grandmother.**

We had our baths in a big galvanized metal washtub in the middle of the kitchen floor. First my sisters and then me; with my mother adding hot water from the teakettle as needed. This wasn't unusual for families in those days. Later, swimming in the quarries solved the bath problem all summer

---

* Many of the Swedish and Finnish "son" names came about as a result of Carl's son becoming Carlson, John's son becoming Johnson, Ander's son becoming Anderson, Hendrick's son becoming Hendrickson, etc.
**In many of the interviews I've conducted for my oral history books this gathering together of families played an important part in the early years of many of the people I've spoken with. No such things as nursing homes back then and people were used to "making do."

long. We'd bring a bar of soap, clean off and dry in the sun. In the winter I'd go to the sauna once a week to avoid the nuisance of being the last one to use the washtub. We went swimming all summer in the quarries, naked of course. No one bothered us as a rule. One day when I was about 12 years old, two young women gave us a shock: jumping in with us completely naked. We were scared and mystified, transfixed I guess, as we had never seen a naked female before. This was a revelation and sort of opened our eyes to the fact that there was an obvious difference we hadn't thought about previously.

We kids used to hang around "Jimmy's Sunrise" (*Jimmy Rantilla*) across from the Finn end of Front Beach. It was a kind of gathering point in those days. Everyone used it as a meeting place to hear the latest gossip or to buy a steamed hot dog for a dime, tonic for a nickel, and a big ice cream cone for a nickel, a double dip or half-pint box for a dime. Jimmy also had a one-armed bandit (*slot machine*) in back: illegal but everyone knew it was there.

I belonged to the Finn Alley gang: Bob Anderson, "Slippery" Wiitanen, Maurice "Mowdy" Ranta, "Ping" Allen, and Billy Toppan. At different times we built huts to hang out and play cards in in the winters. One hut was built just behind the "Rendola", a long apartment house of sorts on Forest Street. Our hut was constructed of cardboard and odds and ends of wood. Early one evening we stoked up the wood-burning stove in the hut and left to go down to the Mill Pond to play "land and sea lubbers" on the ice. We carelessly left the oilcloth curtain drawn down too close to the flue pipe and it ignited the curtain. A neighbor came racing down to the pond after the fire alarm blew in and screamed that our hut was on

fire. We didn't know whether to run toward the fire or away from it; we were so frightened by the possible consequences. We finally went back up and found the hut was a total loss and the firemen watering down the embers. The "Rendola" was painted by Sonny Hooper with used and discarded motor oil as a cheap way of preserving the shingles. The firemen had been afraid the house would ignite from the burning embers of the hut but, fortunately for us, it didn't and we were off that particular hook.

I guess most of us didn't realize that we were poor. We were all in the same boat, so to speak. We really had a wonderful childhood as I look back upon it: carefree, fishing and occasional lobstering, fun at Front Beach, swimming in the quarries, hiking in the woods, trapping, rifle practice, building huts and playing cards. We picked lots of blueberries for pies and muffins, and my mother preserved them for winter use. I also sold them for 20 cents a quart to the non-pickers, which helped out at home. I still love to go up in the woods and pick blueberries. I have been disappointed at the scarcity of berries these past few years. If we have a good season, believe me, I'll be up there picking gallons of them for the freezer, pies, muffins, and blueberry pancakes: I can taste them even as I think about them.

My father was a quarry worker. He worked Steel Derrick and Kenny's pit over near Locust Grove cemetery in Lanesville. In fact, my grandfather was killed in what they called Kenny's pit. I'm not really sure of the accuracy of the story but he was in charge of the blasting. They used a powder line to blow the stone. When they laid down the powder line, my grandfather was the one who lit it and got everybody away from it. A stone fell and kicked a spark right into the powder line and it blew up prematurely and injured him quite badly: he didn't live long after that. Many men were injured in quarry accidents; it was a very dangerous business. There were many cases of what they called "stonecutter's consumption" from inhaling the stone dust. There was no protection to prevent or cure this: no medical insurance or unemployment compensation in those days. Just every man for himself.

My father worked Steel Derrick: one of my grandfathers worked there. And the granite industry folded up not too long after that. The Rogers brothers (*Louie and Harry, owners and proprietors of the Rockport Granite Company*) lived a different life than their workers. The Finns and Swedes and Italians used to fight amongst themselves but were united in their resentment at the distance between themselves and the Rogers brothers. When I was growing up I heard good about the Finns and bad about the Finns: same way with the Swedes. I don't know who drank more, but I think I'd bet on the Finns.

I graduated from Rockport High School in 1936. My first two years of school were in the Legion Hall. The third and fourth years at the George J. Tarr school (*now the Rockport library building*). Up to Broadway for the fifth and sixth grades (*torn down to make way for the present police-fire stations.*) Down to the foot of Broadway to the old junior-senior high school in what are now the High School Apartments. In the Legion Hall (*the Beach Street school*) I used to crawl down to the cellar through the trap door: it's still there in the floor, to fill the coal hod to feed the big pot-belly stove that heated the school.

When I was old enough; about high school age, I went to work for Orren Poole after school and summers doing things like planting potatoes for 30 cents an hour. I turned my earnings over to my mother in order to help pay off our grocery bill at Jack Walima's store. (*Walima's Market, beneath Temperance Hall on Forest Street*) Jack was very good about allowing people who traded with him to charge their groceries, and trusted them to pay their bills. He never harassed them, no matter how long it took. Many of his customers were Finns, like himself and his partner. They delivered groceries for no extra charge and their meat was especially good.

I'm so glad that the old high school wasn't torn down for parking. It would have been such a loss, just as the old Town Hall was a loss. I didn't pretend to be much of a student, hating the times I had to stand up in front of the class to give a book report. Most of us kids in those days weren't trained for public speaking, and we were self-conscious and shy. I was eager to finish school so I could try to find work and help my family.

Martta Somppi lived right across the street from us. Eddie "Minnix" Ranta lived down next to his father's store, the Emil Ranta store. The Contrinos lived across the street for a while, in the house "Ping" moved out of. Lester and Jennie Olson lived down on the corner of King Street. Jennie's maiden name was Toppan and her brother Billy ran with our gang also. "Speelins" Palmquist was in our crowd: his real name was Arthur Houle, and he was quite a character. Jim "Tussie" Riley gave him that name, Speelins. Harold Whittaker and "Rainbow" Johnson used to pal around with us also.

We had a hut down behind Bob Anderson's place on King Street. We spent a lot of time down there. We used to fish in the Mill Pond, off that low stone wall behind Bob's house. We used to get shiners a foot long out of there: catch 'em with a small hook. There was another ice house (*other than Reuben Norwood's on the easterly side of the pond*) just below Bob's house (*the westerly side of the pond*). There seemed to be millions of shiners in there and rather than throw the fish back we'd throw them over the fence into the hen yard. We did that for a couple of weeks, you know, feed the hens, they were always hungry and they'd gobble them down. Until Mrs. Anderson (*Hilda Anderson, Bob's mother*) asked us if we were throwing fish into the hen yard. We said, yuh. She said we'd better stop it because the eggs were starting to taste like fish. We loved that pond. We always played around the pond: trapped and skated in the winter, and fished in the summer.

We used to play down in the factory yard (*now Millbrook Meadow*). Called the factory yard for the old, abandoned isinglass factory that used to stand next to today's waterfall. I remember when that building burned (*in 1932*). We (our Finn alley gang) were in there around five o'clock that night, up on the third floor. I hope Joe Thibeault doesn't come back to haunt me for this: he had bought the place to make a miniature golf course in the factory yard. There were three or four of us in there, Albert Tuck was with us too. We used to go in there and chase the pigeons around; pigeons flew in and out all the time. And of course, some of the guys smoked.

We left there and went down through town, to see if we could start some trouble somewhere and when the alarm blew in, someone said it was the factory. We got scared, afraid they were going to blame us. We stayed down on Bearskin Neck for a while until things quieted down a little bit. Then we came up Beach Street and up through the old cemetery across from Front Beach, and watched it burn from the top of the hill at the end of Mill Lane. There were a ton of sparks flying and people were wetting down their roofs along Mill Lane.

My mother gave me the third degree, asking if we had been in there: she knew we hung out in there. Everything used in the making of isinglass was still there: it looked like everyone had died at the controls, so to speak. The belts were still there, pulleys on the engines in the boiler room: the fires had just been left, the coals were still in the furnace. The place was wide open. Nobody gave a damn about it. I remember the awful smells of the old leather belts still in place. The only thing left after the fire were the bricks in the foundation.

Not long after the fire they wanted to clean the place up, get rid of that old red brick foundation. Joe Thibeault came along and offered me and Speelins two dollars apiece to pick up all those bricks and bring them around to the road, where they could throw them on a truck. I remember I had my little cart and carried them out to the road but Speelins wouldn't do his share: I had to growl at him to get him to do his part. He took the two dollars but I was doing all the work. Bill MacDonald, Joe Thibeault, and there was a French guy living down in back of the Pete Curtis's waiting station on Main Street, were partners in that miniature golf course but there wasn't any money to be made at that stuff in those days. After that folded the town took the land over and it stayed public property.

Down in the Union cemetery on Union Lane they had those two rounded off, in ground tomb-like places where they put people in the winter when they couldn't dig in the ground. They had those big iron doors on them with a hasp for locking them when they had people in there. But when there was nobody in there, as I recall, they had a wooden pin to keep the door closed. We used to play around there quite a bit, never malicious. We heard some of the older guys talking about making their own wine and we thought we'd experiment on it. So where did we make it? . . . inside one of those "lay away" units.

We tried to make elderberry wine. There were four or five of us and we didn't know anything about making wine but we did know you had to strain it. We did that alright and put it in a firkin to let it work, but we didn't leave it in long enough. So when we put it into bottles it became like a hand grenade. We asked this certain guy to come and taste it. It was still working. We played the big shots; come and try our brew. He had a brand new outfit on. He lifted the bottle and it blew up right in his face: wine all over him. It ruined his outfit.

We had borrowed, without her knowledge, a brand new aluminum kettle my mother had just bought to do the straining into. When we went to clean it out it wouldn't clean. It stayed purple: I didn't know what to do about it, I couldn't bring it home, I'd a got shot. My old gent asked what I had been doing with this thing and I tried to make nothing of it. "We just made a little wine in it. I can't bring it in because Ma will give me hell." He got me off the hook by saying that he'd taken it down to the Legion or somewhere and that's where the staining had happened.

We locked Francis Haskell in one of those storage units once. On this day we were scrapping with Lawrence Jodrey and Francis Haskell. And somehow we managed to get Frank inside what we used to call the tomb. We put a stick in the hasp and locked him in there and went off and left him. Naturally he hollered like a banshee and pounded on that iron door. I don't remember why we put him in there but we weren't going to let him out. We went on across Mill Pond and watched for a while and I think it was either Lawrence Jodrey who finally let him out or his pounding on the door snapped the wooden peg in the hasp.

Up in back of what we used to call Manning's Woods, or Manning Park, across Granite Street from the top of Forest Street, Saturdays and Sundays these old timers, Finns and Swedes, would go up into the woods where they had the biggest round flat rock they could find. Around this big rock were about eight smaller flat rocks that they could sit on, and they'd play poker there. Not too many feet up into the woods was where this clearing was. They'd sit there and play cards: I suppose there was a certain amount of scrapping and a certain amount of drinking. Us kids made it a habit, in the evening, when things had quieted down, to go up there and scrounge around the weeds, looking for money that had dropped off the table . . . loose change that had not made it into a pot. We'd go up there Saturday night and sometimes we'd go up there Sunday night to pick up a few coins. They just played for pennies, nickels and dimes: things were tough in those days. The old gent went up and played poker. I used to ask him about it but he was very tight lipped: he didn't want my mother to know anything about it.

After high school I applied to the Beverly Trade School to study auto mechanics. That didn't last very long. I went by train for a few weeks up there but I wasn't all that interested: I really don't know what I did it for. I was there for about a month when I got a job offer at the Hotel Bradford in Boston. Ray "Cookie" Kultti was "Fat" Johnson's half brother, Fat was a great left handed pitcher for the Town Team, and they were working for the Hotel Bradford in the engineering and maintainence department. They gave me a job: my old man kind of put a bug in their ear. He didn't want me to hang around Rockport, he wanted me to get out and get to work where there was something going on. All we had locally was pick-up crappy little jobs: cleaning out hen houses and stuff like that. To make a buck or two we used to go trapping: we got a buck and a half for a pelt. We used to trap up behind Mill Pond: me, Bob Anderson, "Ping" Allen, Maurice Ranta, we were all from that same Forest Street neighborhood.

(At this point in our interview both Pat and his wife Norma reminisced a bit about their 60 year marriage and how Pat had prevailed upon Harold Whittaker to introduce him to Norma on Front Beach one day. All very proper.)

So after I went to work at the Bradford I found I could visit Norma in Melrose quite frequently. After three years of dating we were married on April 9, 1939. We had five children. We lost David Alan as an infant. Our oldest, Steven, passed away two years ago. Our youngest daughter, Lisa, passed away September 15, 1998 after a three year slege of terrible suffering as a quadriplegic with complications from diabetes. It is so difficult to lose a child: the sadness lingers on forever.

But we have had good times as well as sad ones. We are grateful for the many happy memories over the years. We are blessed by having the care of Lisa's son Nicholas, who is now 12 years old. He makes life worth liv-ing, taking after his Mom in so many ways: he's talented and creative as Lisa was, and resembles her.

We were married for five years when I had to go into the Army. I did my basic training in the horrific summer heat of Camp Blanding, Florida. I was given an emergency leave home because Norma, who was pregnant with our first child, became dangerously ill. David Alan was born but lived only a few days. I had to return to my outfit after his funeral, leaving my seriously sick wife behind.

At Fort Dix in New Jersey we were given our rifles and our orders to go overseas on the U.S.S.Wakefield. We landed in LeHarve, France and rode across our portion of France in the old 40 and 8* railroad cars, winding up in Metz. We joined our outfit in Luxembourg and prepared to join the Battle of the Bulge on the Siegfried Line. We were driven to the battle in half tracks. Halfway there a large mortar shell dropped right in the middle of our troops, causing havoc and many deaths: we knew then that the Germans were active. We were pretty much in the midst of mortar and shell fire all along the Our River. Our platoon leader was killed almost at once by an egg mine as we went through a German mine field.

Then our squad leader and many others were killed or wounded and at this time I was wounded by shrapnel. The next day it was dug out of me on a table in an old farm house we were in after having been driven out of our position. There were only a few of us left, and we had to move the more seriously wounded to safety. We had no choice but to leave our dead comrades where they

---

*So named in World War I for railroad transportation; signifying the carrying capacity of each car: 40 men and 8 horses.

lay. When we heard German patrols we threw hand grenades to keep them from getting too close. It was pitiful to hear the wounded scream in pain.

We got new replacements and were told to stay where we were and not to advance until further orders. We dug into the ground as best we could to avoid the gunfire. The men were being hit all around me; many wounded and killed.

Many months later, in June, we were told to still stay in our foxholes when we saw our tanks moving ahead and they kept on going. We knew then that there had been a breakthrough and suspected that the war was nearly over. The day we crossed the Rhine we dug in on the German side and celebrated with wine captured on our way into Germany. That night a few ME 109's strafed us and, thanks to the wine, most of us didn't know we had been attacked.

After the German surrender, slave laborers and displaced persons were taken by our outfit to Liege, Belgium. A dozen GI's acted as infantry guards on each train to protect these former German prisoners from German activity along the rail lines. Even though we still rode in the 40 and 8's with their square wheels and French engineers, it was good to get out of camp.

We also helped to clear the Buchenwald area of SS troops and were then able to free the final prisoners from the Buchenwald camp. Many were dying of starvation and tuberculosis, or were terribly wounded, having had no medical care. It was incredibly shocking to see the way these people had been mistreated. Our whole battalion was taken through Buchenwald as witnesses to this horrible happening and lack of humanity.

After Buchenwald we bivouacked in fields near a town and almost immediately began training to go to China, Burma and India, where the fighting was still going on. We were scheduled to go home for a month's leave before being shipped to Texas before entering the war with Japan. Fortunately for us, the day we sailed into New York harbor the war with Japan ended, thanks to the use of the atomic bombs. We were sent to Camp Shelby in Mississippi and from there to Texas, where Norma joined me. Eight months later, on April 11, 1946, I received an honorable discharge and we left almost immediately for home by bus. We stopped to rest and sightsee along the way and were overwhelmed by the treatment we got in each city where we stopped. The uniform was respected everywhere, and we were given free rooms in the best hotels; something we have never forgotten.

After the war, I returned to my job with the Gas Company, which had been held open for me. We came back to live year 'round in Rockport in June, 1971. I commuted to work for eight years, and retired at age 60 after 38 years with the same company. It was such a good feeling to come back to my roots. All the family felt good about it. Two of our children were still in school and they graduated from Rockport High. Rockport has changed in recent years, no longer the quaint little town I grew up in. Everyone has discovered it's charm and beauty and we have been unundated with newcomers, many building palatial homes on every available spot of land. But the nostalgia remains and I still love to go hiking in the woods, visiting my old haunts and picking blueberries whenever nature obliges with a good crop.

The first portion of this entry was taped on May 7, 1998 at the Hendrickson home on Granite Street in Pigeon Cove. Second and third additions have been handwritten by Norma as told by Pat. Pat didn't particularly want to speak about his war experiences, thinking it might be misinterpreted as a form of braggadocio but I prevailed upon him to speak of his World War II military experiences. Without these and similar reminiscences we might forget just how awful war can be. I think such individual records should be kept before us at all times.

Standing near Curtis News store, the "waiting station" for years along Main Street toward the junction with School Street probably after the same snowfall seen on page 68. Note the large elm tree in the foreground: one of many that once graced our streets.

Inner harbor showing two fishing sloops moored to T Wharf. The former freezer on the end of the wharf can be seen on the right. The freezer was built in 1918 and burned down in 1923.

MARTHA KETCHOPULOS POHAS
(Mrs. George Pohas)

Born in Rockport in 1916. Her husband George, the well known and loved Gloucester physician, died in 2000.

MY FATHER, JAMES, came to Gloucester in 1901. He moved to Rockport in 1902. He had two brothers here ahead of him and he came over from Greece to visit them. He was in his twenties at the time and couldn't speak English at all. He came ashore at Ellis Island where they put a tag on him that said Gloucester, Mass. They put him on a train and he had to change trains in Boston from South to North Station and he somehow managed to do this without knowing the language and made it to Gloucester. His brothers lived on Rogers Street and my father had a letter he had brought from Greece with him which he showed to a man on the street and the man was good enough to take him to his brothers' place. The brothers were not married at the time so there were three young Greek bachelors then living in Gloucester.

The first two brothers were selling fruits from pushcarts. The three of them did that for a couple of years and then my father bought the house in Rockport *(the place across from the depot on Railroad Avenue; the house the train failed to stop one day at the end of the railroad track from Boston, crossed the road and smashed into)*. We went down to Broadway from there and lived above the market on the corner of Broadway and School Street. I had two brothers, "Ketchy" and "Razz": I was between the two boys. We were the only Greek family in town for many years. We didn't feel any prejudice

against our nationality. As a matter of fact the people in town respected us and shopped at our market. Rather than be discriminated against we were taken in as a part of the town right away.

We eventually bought the farm on Poole's Lane (now the Millbrook Park housing for the elderly project) from Bill Evans to grow the vegetables we sold in the market. We also had chickens there in two hen houses. During the war (World War II) that was good because they didn't ration chickens and we sold thousands of them. Before we grew our own vegetables we had to go into Boston three times a week to get our produce. Before my father got a truck he used to take the train to Boston to make his orders and they'd ship it down here on the boats. After he got his truck he got up at three in the morning to go to the city and be back at the market by ten. While he was on the road my mother, my two brothers and I ran the store. We all lived over the market but my brother John lived up on the farm when he got married. That land went from Main Street down Poole's Lane to the railroad tracks and from the Lane to Railroad Avenue: we owned a lot of land there. I was born in Rockport in the house on Railroad Avenue that was hit by the train. I graduated from Rockport High School and then got married to Doctor Pohas.

The train hit the house on a Saturday night when we were at the movies in the Town Hall. A Mr. Zetes, a Greek man, ran the movies at that time. Somebody came in to the Hall and said that there had been an accident and told of a train hitting a building. I said that it sounded like our building but it could have been next door. When we went home everybody was there. No one was killed, anyway. The waitress fell down cellar and my uncle opened the door to see what was going on and saw the train there. There was nobody in the restaurant at the time: they used to wait for that train to come in before closing up. (*The first floor of the Ketchopulos Railroad Avenue building was a restaurant and they lived above it. Martha's uncle John Jeanopulos ran the restaurant, which served an American menu, and he did all the cooking. He later opened Johnny's Restaurant on Main Street in the space formerly occupied for his tailor/haberdashery shop by the author's grandfather, Arthur Oker: where he, Arthur, was brutally murdered in 1932*). My uncle ran the restaurant and after the accident he came to live with us for a few years and after that we had the farm and he had the restaurant on Main Street.

(*At this point in the interview I turned to Doctor Pohas for the following information*) I'm retired now: I practiced for fifty years, that's long enough. I retired in 1986, I'm 87 years old. We've been married since 1935. Martha's father was a hard worker, a tremendous person. Martha's mother was a very capable lady, a very intellectual lady, I think she had more understanding of human beings; their thoughts, their desires, than a college graduate. One of the first things I noticed about her when I first met her was her tremendous ability to know people.

Our wedding in Rockport was on a Sunday and they closed Broadway and School Street; no traffic at all. We got married in the house above the market. Their market was really a gourmet market: they had the best of everything. You couldn't find some of the stuff they had in there in

Boston. People came from all over to shop there. Even after I went into the practice of medicine I used to go to work in the market on Wednesdays because that was my day off from my practice. I really enjoyed working there; I enjoyed the people, the customers. The only non-Greek person who worked in the market was Helen Poole, Helen Church; she was the book keeper there. She was a marvelous lady, hard working, conscientious, honest as the day is long.

Pohas is a Greek name: it was changed a bit from the original at Ellis Island but it's still pretty much what it was. Poulos on the end of a Greek name means the son of: so Ketchopulos means the son of Ketch. When I was in medical school I found many aspects of medicine easy to understand because most Western medicine is based on the Greek, there are so many Greek names and definitions . . . I didn't have to memorize the Greek words.

(*Back to Martha*) I walked to school when we lived on Railroad Avenue and that was hard, we used to walk home for lunch. It was much easier when we moved to Broadway, we were right across the street from the school. I used to take care of my brothers down on Broadway, I'd help get them dressed. I remember that Mr. Evans had two dogs (big shepards) that ran down and chased us along Railroad Avenue when we walked back and forth to and from school.

I was sixteen when we bought the farm. We kids drove down the lane in our Model T Ford: we took turns driving and it was all right because nobody was there. That's how I learned to drive when I was fourteen, down Poole's Lane. We'd drive down to the brook (now called Millbrook). We also had lambs on the farm; we ate the lambs. We'd barbeque them on spits over a fire for hours.

My father got married in the Town Hall in 1912. My mother came over from Greece. She came from my father's home town, Tripoli. My father's mother and sister went over to Greece and brought my mother and my uncle to this country. My uncle stayed here for a couple of years and then he went and joined the circus. He sold hot dogs at the circus. He came back to visit us and my mother made him stay and he became part of our family circle. I remember my mother looking out the window toward the depot and she saw her brother getting off the train; the first time she knew he was coming.

We have three daughters: our oldest daughter is retired, our second daughter is teaching at the West Parish school, and our youngest daughter is out in Los Angeles, California. We have five grandchildren and ten great-grandchildren, and they are all here in Essex county, between here and Hamilton.

We had just a small flower garden out back and we had my nephew (contractor Jim Ketchopulos) turn the soil over and I had a vegetable farm out there: string beans, cauliflower, celery, lettuce, zucchini, tomatoes, a lot of things. I called it a garden but my husband called it a farm. I started it about ten years ago (*Martha would have been in her early seventies*) but it didn't last long, only about three years.

We go to the Greek church up in Ipswich: we don't have enough local Greeks to warrant a Cape Ann church. The Cape Ann Greek community is now actually smaller than it once was. They intermarried, some died, others moved away, there's very few Greeks here now.

Two schooners moored to the North side of T wharf with the fish freezer looming between the masts and rigging. Not many pleasure craft in Rockport harbor at this time.

MAFALDA "MUFFIE" POLLONI

Muffie is a maiden lady who was born in 1909 and has lived all her life in Pigeon Cove; enjoying every minute of it. Sad to say, Muffie died before this book made it into print. She is missed.

MY PARENTS LIVED and met near Carrara, which was in northern Italy, east of Genoa. It was the home of famous marble quarries *(favored by Michelangelo)*, however; my father did not work in marble. If you ever saw how they quarried that marble you'd die: they did it the hard way; by hand. The landscape of New England is why my folks felt so much at home in Rockport. Corneda was my mother's home town. I was lucky enough to go there later in my life. When I went to get my passport for the trip the clerk asked me if I intended to go again. I said, "Heavens no, I'm lucky to go now." So he put down "maybe." And I returned twice more.

My mother was about 21 years old when she came to this country with her mother and her brother. My mother and father had met in Italy but she came over first and he followed her later: it was very romantic. My father chased my mother to America. My father knew he had to get out of his home town because there were too many mouths to feed at home. He had completed his compulsory military service. They were a farming family and it wasn't too easy a life. They also ran a mill where they ground people's corn and chestnuts for flour. I think that same farm still goes.

My mother and her family originally settled in Branford, Connecticut, I don't know why. My mother was nearly 21 years old at that time. Her mother used to cry all the time because she didn't make an easy transition from Italy to this country. My grandmother couldn't stand those "smelly American cats" *(skunks)*. She actually did go back to Italy but eventually came back to America to be with her husband. My maternal grandfather had been a caretaker on an estate in Italy. His employers told him that if he didn't like America he could return to Italy and have his old job back; I guess he was very well thought of. He did go back and did get his old job back and he was happy.

When we lived down in the woods off Curtis Street my mother made all our clothes. We had pigs, two cows and some hens. We grew lots of vegetables there. We also picked blueberries and sold them and dug up and sold dandelion greens. We loved the greens, they made a good meal. We put olive oil on them. There were apple and pear trees all around the place. We used to to get in and play with the pigs. We would wash the pigs up; oh, didn't they love it! We had a brook and we'd get right into the brook. In the winter we'd skate down the brook to John Martin's store on Stockholm Avenue and go right into the store with our skates on. One year my mother planted peanuts all around the house and how they come up! She hid them to dry out and we never saw them again; we never knew what happened to them. Maybe a mouse came into the cellar and ate them but we never knew. My mother was sad about it and I didn't blame her.

While we were there in the woods an uncle and aunt came over from Italy. My folks had written them that they should come to America; that it was beautiful, and they could start a new life here and things would be so different. They arrived in Rockport at night at the Rockport depot. Charles Balzarini *(from the Curtis Street Balzarinis)* had a wooden Ford automobile wagon of some sort and he met them at the station. My aunt said that when she stepped out of the wagon in Pigeon Cove . . . " what did I do? I stepped in a cow flap!" Welcome to America. They stayed with us for a while until they got a house. I think they moved to Lanesville.

We were still living in the woods when we had the great flu epidemic of 1918.* I remember we all got sick. This past summer *(1999)* reminded me of it. Everything was drying up because of the drought. But finally the Red Cross did come down to see us. That's when we were introduced to fish chowder and tapioca pudding. We were so hungry we were glad to get it. I was very sick. I hemorrhaged through my nose. My 12 year old sister took care of my mother and father who were down with the flu. We couldn't get a doctor for a long time.

Finally a doctor came and he packed my nose. I was better and slept that night but early the next morning I started to sneeze and blew out the packing. My mother woke up and saw all the blood and fell on the floor. My sisters and I talk about this every once in a while. We had a bottle of some kind of liquor tucked behind a trunk that was supposed to settle your stomach . . . we used it for everything. I jumped out of bed, grabbed the bottle and took a swig. The doctor came in later after I had stopped bleeding: I was a tough thing! That flu epidemic was awful. They even had tents outside the Addison Gilbert and Haskins hospitals. People were dying left and right. Everyone in our family survived the flu.

We went to school in Pigeon Cove in the Reed school. I only went to elementary school; I was not a scholar. I wrote like a wild rabbit. I did have a little problem: I was hard of hearing and still am. I would have liked to go to art school; my elementary teacher, Miss Lurvey, said that art was all I was good at. One day my real art teacher, Miss Tuttle, said she had a surprise for us as she put an apple on the table and as we watched, a mouse came out of it. Then we drew it.

We used to bring my father's lunch to him when he worked in the Halibut Point quarry. It was only a short walk from our house on Granite Street. We had moved by this time. When it was working the quarry was some sight! Two boys were killed on the grout pile next to the quarry many years later. They were climbing on it and the moving rocks caused an avalanche. it shifted: I can still see the feet of those boys sticking out of the pile!

We used to go up to the Halibut Point pit to swim after it closed and filled with water. There was a ledge to get down to the water and we could walk off of it. I never went over my head: I would drown. If I got over my head I'd panic. We couldn't swim that good. There were many people who drowned around here, some on thin ice, like the Balestraci boy, only fourteen years old. He and a friend were skating when the ice crashed and down he went.

My father worked in the quarries and

---

* The disease had entered the country through the Port of Boston and by the end of that year 929 cases had been reported to the Rockport Board of Health, 18 of these were fatal. 86 cases of other diseases hit the town in 1918, nine of these fatal. Not a very healthy year for the town.

the Tool Company but he couldn't stand the awful hard work in both those places. He was not suited for heavy work. He did odd jobs here and there, working in gardens for people. He was a wonderful gardener.

When they had the strike at the Rockport Granite Company my father was rather depressed that things were so bad, with strikes and labor unrest. He told us not to go down the street because it was so dangerous. He told us not to wear our red hair ribbons for fear that someone might think we were communists. This happened in 1922 and the strike went on until 1925.

Every spring we all had a good dose of castor oil. The dandelion greens were also our spring tonic. My mother made dandelion wine but she'd never drink it herself. She loved to serve it. We all had grape wine. There was always a bottle of wine on the table at dinner time. She once in a while would add it to our soup "for iron" but I said that I didn't want that old wine in my soup.

We used to take our cows to Pigeon Hill, right by what's now called Landmark Lane. We worked two fields on the Hill and the Balzarinis had some fields there too. We used to visit with them as we took the cows up and back. We brought them home over the road but we couldn't do that today. One day we wanted to make some fudge but had no milk so we milked a cow in the pasture. My mother said it was strange that that cow didn't give her as much milk as usual that day.

My mother had one pet cow, a Guernsey, and she called her Daisy. She was a pretty cow and gave rich milk. Mrs. Cusick always wanted the milk from that cow and she knew when she didn't get that milk. I thought Daisy was the laziest, dirtiest cow but she was my mother's favorite. She washed her every time before she milked her.

That cow was so lazy she didn't even get up to do her business. We kept the cows in our little barn and we'd have plays in the barn and everything. I don't know anyone who had more going on than we did. When we lived on Pasture Road near Charles Cleaves' big barn there were gardens all the way up the Pigeon Hill slope: all kinds of vegetables. Charles Cleaves rented a part of his barn to Charles Balzarini, of the Curtis Street Balzarinis. My father rented the other half of the barn. I think the Balzarinis used to make hay up on the Hill also. That land belonged to Ezra Cleaves; he owned a lot of land. The main Cleaves house (*12 Pasture Road, where the Garlicks presently reside*) was a beautiful house.

We had a horse and old wagon at one time. We got the axles for the wagon from the Tool Company. One year we all got shovels and Papa drove the wagon to where we loaded it up with ashes and spread it next to the Pigeon Cove school on Story Street (*the present Pingree Park, with a baseball diamond and tennis courts*). We spread it where the kids play ball now because it was low land there. Those were days when everybody helped everybody else.

We loved the Village Improvement Society "Days". These were annual events. The Society had fairs at Chester Story's place on Granite Street and the whole Cove took part. One year Rose Balzarini had a collie dog who had puppies and Rose brought her and her puppies to the fair. For either one cent or ten cents, I forget which, you had a peek at the puppies nursing. Those fairs were something; they even had games for the kids. The Society did so much for Pigeon Cove.

What with the quarry workers strike and everything together, not being able to really handle heavy work, my father got sick and died in 1922. My mother was 35 years old when he died. People were so nice to us. They didn't pity us, they just wanted to help us. The oldest child was fifteen and the youngest one was about six. People knew my mother was a widow lady and willing to go out and do any work people needed. Shortly before my father died we had moved to 281 Granite Street. Charles and Lottie Parady lived upstairs.

I left school from the seventh grade and my mother said if I left school I was going to have to go to work. I went to work for a family in Gloucester as a "general": I was told that was what people like me were called in England. I stayed overnight because it was expensive going back and forth on the bus. I got Thursday and Sunday afternoons off. I worked with the lady of the house and it was an education.

After I got through with the Gloucester job I was just sort of drifting around and one of the ladies I babysat for said she thought I ought to go to cooking school. So I did. That was something. I went to the vocational school in Boston. I went to Boston three days a week and worked the other days, which paid for the school and train tickets. I got where I loved the city and got a lot out of it. We worked hard but had a nice time. I walked home from the Rockport depot every night, scared to death.

After the school I did get a job as a chef but I didn't like it. It was for the Wemyss family (*who ran the Yankee Clipper Inn in Pigeon Cove*). They were easy people to work for but I was supposed to do the hiring and firing and all and I wasn't a good boss. I spent 35 years in different hotels and inn kitchens as "head cook" and did like that work.

We used to walk to the Sacred Heart Church in Lanesville for our church: walk all the way over and all the way back. In the winter that was some cold walk. Churches these days seem to cater to people with problems. Problems are ancient history to me: I've had plenty of them. When I have problems, that's when I have to say my prayers.

My mother would help anybody, sometimes even if she didn't get paid. We did come to this house (*269 Granite Street in Pigeon Cove*) to help out a Mrs. Pike. Mr. and Mrs. Pike had this place built. They lived here and had chickens, raspberries and apples and I think used to sell them. Mr. Pike was the superintendent of the cemetery in Lanesville. After Mr. Pike died Mrs. Pike married Mr. Godey. Her son Robert Pike in the meantime came home to live following "sleeping sickness" he got on the job at Lincoln Motors. Robert hired my mother full time to come and help out. When Mrs. Godey died Robert asked my mother and our family to move in because by then he required around the clock care and I've been here ever since.

My life in this house has been very good. For that matter, I've had a good life all along. I've had the good luck to have spent my whole life in Rockport. It has been a great journey these 91 years.

MARY PUCCI COUCHMAN

Mary was born on Dec. 23, 1922 in the Pigeon Cove area which is presently known as Folly Cove but at one time was called Blubber Hollow.

"I've been a pediatrician for 30 years. I got through my early schooling quickly and went to Simmons on a scholarship where I majored in science. I worked for the State Department of Public Health for two years and salted my money away, so with that and some further scholarship money and some loans I got through my medical training very nicely. I was lucky. My husband (also an MD) and I practiced in Iowa. He was a Mid-Westerner who studied at Harvard and didn't like much of the snobbery he found there."

MY PEOPLE CAME to Rockport as stone cutters. My mother and father were from Lucca, which is about 14 miles from Pisa and 48 miles west of Florence. These folks were from the foothills of the Carrara, *(home of the world's finest marble.)* They didn't stray very far from their home villages what with the lack of any real transportation system. They knew their local area very well but it was a very limited area. My father had met my mother, who was from another village, close by to his home town. These small villages had their own particular dialects and could be identified by them. They observed the same local holidays and they had their own specific dishes which reflected their individual culinary tastes.

My father came to this country at the turn of the century and was here for about three years before he went back to Italy and got my mother. My father was born in 1877 so he was quite grown up when he came here. He came through Ellis Island. He first worked for six months in a New York hotel as a waiter and hated it. He then joined with a group of workers who were going to work in a limestone quarry in Sandusky, Ohio and worked there for about a year. The company had a branch in Delaware and they sent my father there and it was from there that he went back to bring my mother here, which resulted in my having some siblings who were born in Delaware. He had had his eye on her back home and had been writing to her, finally talking her into coming to this country to be with him.

Then the company sent him on to open a new granite quarry in the Folly Point section of Gloucester. The quarry was up there where the Slades (those of the codfish aristocracy*) used to live. They were very shallow quarries but being next to those nice flat ledges sloping down to the ocean they could easily load the granite onto barges. My father didn't actually cut the stones: he didn't cut paving stones and the like. He was not a finisher, he was a blaster-detonator and a steam drill operator. The finishers in the quarries were usually Northern Italians and they sculpted the friezes and statuary that were sometimes called for to made from Cape Ann granite. A lot of those workers came from around Verona, Romeo and Juliet country.

These quarries were not Rockport Granite or Pigeon Hill Granite Companies or Leonard Johnson's. Many of them were owned by individual entrepreneurs. But the Folly Point quarry didn't do all that well. My

---

*A term used to describe those who became well off through the fishing industry.

father thought it was probably because they hadn't made it deep enough and it wasn't all that profitable. But they did erect a barracks for the workers there. My mother and Mrs. Bianchini were the cooks for about forty Folly Point quarry workers; among them a group of Turks. The owners brought in some Turks to work the granite. I don't know exactly how they were recruited or brought to this country but I do know that they were Muslims and they wore turbans. They dressed in flowing white robes and hated it here because it was so cold. I'm assuming they were Turks: my mother called them Turks. They also hated their food: being unable to have their traditional foods prepared for them. They bowed to the East several times a day to say their prayers. I think they only stayed on the job for about a year.

I can't put a name on the company that started this Folly Point quarry. I remember my father calling it the New Company; separating it from having anything to do with the Rockport Granite Company. Those workers got their drinking water from that scuzzy pond right at the edge of the Locust Grove cemetery. I know about that because my father came down with typohid fever and my mother always said it was the water. He was in the hospital for 26 days (*a far cry from today's hospital stays*).

The Folly Cove pier is entirely man made. Before the pier was built, In the whaling days, apparently they hauled whales ashore in the natural rather open inlet about where the lobster restaurant is today to be flensed* out and it became known as Blubber Hollow. I'm probably the last living native of Blubber Hollow. I was born in a little house in Blubber Hollow which was

moved over to Curtis Street in the thirties, down next to the Carter place near what we called the dam in the Pine Pit swampy hollow. During Prohibition some bootleggers set a house afire up in the woods to keep the local gendarmes busy while they landed a load of whiskey down in the Folly.

After the Folly Point quarry my parents rented a house from the Rockport Granite Company. At one time my father owned that house nearly on the Town Line between Rockport and Gloucester at the far end of Granite Street. My mother had said that she was pretty sick and tired of living in those barracks and if my father didn't provide better housing for her she was going back to Italy.

While she was pregnant with her third child on the Cape the company was ready to send my father back to Delaware. They moved their workers around at will in those days. My mother balked at this and said that they had to put some roots down here. She had two babies while living in those barracks. So he bought a house on Granite Street. After two years there my mother insisted they get another house because it was so cold and drafty in this made over fish shack. She was 41 when I was born: I was one of those change of life babies.

My father sold the place and they then rented a house down in Blubber Hollow . . . right down in the Hollow, where the trolley used to turn around. It was owned by the Rockport Granite Company: all that land was owned by the Rockport Granite Company. That's the house where I was born and it stood at the present day 330 Granite Street. All those houses up the hill toward Rockport from the Hollow are relatively

*Flense: to strip off a whale's blubber or skin.

new. There was a field in that area when I was young and Antone Balzarini used it as a pasture. I think my father continued to work in local quarries in Bay View and Lanesville, but not for the Rockport Granite Company. I'm a little vague about exactly who he might have worked for, maybe even Leonard Johnson in the Pigeon Cove woods behind Steel Derrick quarry.

When the quarry workers went on strike, seeking better pay and working conditions (*they were very poorly paid*) the Company brought in scabs creating a great deal of unrest in the industry. My father didn't like the resulting tensions and decided to get out of quarry work and wound up working for the Cape Ann Tool Company for almost 18 years. He was about 56 when he retired from the Tool Company and then ran a little vegetable truck garden. He also did people's landscaping. He was a great trimmer, having learned something about topiary when he was a young boy growing up.

When I was about eleven years old and my father had left the Granite Company and was at the Tool Company he bought a house next to the Gott house over on Gott Avenue, the Holmes place now. I really grew up on Gott Avenue. That's where I got my Anglo-Saxon surrogate mother, Lizzie McLellan. I was with her a great deal and this was nice for me, an immigrant child, picking up all sorts of different cultural influences. We used the Italian language in our home: my father thinking that we should do this to keep our heritage alive and when we got into school we'd pick up the English. I was the youngest so I had picked up much English, a lot of it from Lizzie McLellan, who always spoke English with me. She told me that when I was two or three years old I'd come to her babbling with stories about some chicken in the chicken yard (we all kept chickens in Pigeon Cove) or some such happening that I'd start out in English but usually wound up in Italian. Lizzie McLellan's maiden name was Orne, an old Rockport family; her son Howard still lives in Pigeon Cove.

Lizzie was a very smart woman with a tremendous fund of knowledge. She was a marvelous gardener with a great deal of herbal and botanical information. She knew all the astral constellations and was a rich source of general information which she freely passed on to us. She was a natural teacher. I remember she'd gather us the day before Memorial Day and we'd cut lilacs and iris and put them in buckets of water. Then the next day we'd trudge up to Locust Grove cemetery and place them on the graves. Even here she taught us things; like not walk on the graves when in a cemetery and to be quiet there. Knowing Lizzie McLellan was a very enriching experience. She was a great role model. In those days we were taught to call our elders "aunt" or "uncle" as a sign of respect. Lizzie McLellan was always Aunt Lizzie.

My father had no Social Security to ease his later years but he always lived very modestly and at one time owned two houses in the area. He was essentially a blue collar worker. He fathered five kids and you can't put much aside with that many to care for. If my mother needed a new refrigerator my brother would go out and buy her one. We all pitched in to take care of the family: that was another generation. My oldest sister never married so she stayed home with our parents.

It's interesting to note that most Italians never changed their names when they came to this country; they were quite independent and proud of their heritage. I remember after World War II ended and the Italians were perceived as going Communist and presented a threat to us. My father said they'd never toe the line for Communism or Russia: not to worry about it. He said they were no threat to democracy.

I went to school in Pigeon Cove; the Story school. But I went to the first grade in Phillips Avenue school *(which is the large, rather square building across the intersection from the Ralph Waldo Emerson Inn: now a private residence.)* There I was the youngest in my family going to school with all these other school kids and I was sick a good deal of the time. All my siblings had experienced many childhood diseases at home and had built up an immunity but I had no immunity to anything, so caught about everything that first year and lost nearly seven weeks of my first school year. I then went to the "new school", the Story School on Story Street, and stayed there through the eighth grade. When they closed the Story school in the nineteen eighties I had a grandson in the first grade in that school, so I told him that I had opened it and he had closed it.

When I was a youngster the Pigeon Cove woods were laced with paths and grout* piles next to the small motions** that are now filled with water and some have even been landscaped by the present owners. We thought of them as woodland eyesores back then. Halibut Point was considered particularly ugly, with its piles of grout and rubble as well as many of their old rusting machines and tools. In recent years these sites have been cleaned up, with some new plantings which cover up these old scars.

We did a lot of blueberrying in the summer. We could sell them to the summer boarders over on the Avenues for 25 cents a quart and that was considered big money back then. You'd find your own "best spot" for berries but you didn't tell anyone else about it. I used to pick right in poison ivy patches because I wasn't allergic to it. We also picked blackberries and our mother would mix them in with blueberries for a pie and sometimes squeeze them and add the juices to our drinking water because the water was terrible in August. We didn't have all the filtering devices for our water that they have today.

Most of us preferred our swimming in the quarries because the water was a little warmer than at the beaches. We'd go ocean swimming and picnicking at Halibut Point from those flat ledges sloping into the water and rinse the salt off in the quarry on the way home. I remember my father telling me later on that I shouldn't walk up around the quarry because a man had bought it and was going to make a park of some kind out of it. Some people seem to resent that the area has been turned into a State Park but I recall that at one time there was fear of condominiums being built there and I think a State Park is more desirable than more condos.

My house (236 Granite Street) was once a part of the Babson estate, which included the present Old Farm Inn. I've heard that when David Babson's children married he'd give each of them a piece of land from that large estate. This house was a

*Grout: the unusable granite chunks produced in the quarrying process.
** Motions: descriptive names for small, sometimes one man, shallow borings into the ubiquitous Cape Ann granite ledges.

summer house for one of his daughters. In 1936 a book by Naomi Lane Babson "The Yankee Bodleys" was published. This book was hotly discussed because although the book was supposedly fictional it was based upon the Babson tribe and there were many people still around who could identify who she wrote about. Some people were interested and others were hostile: it all depended upon how closely related to the Babsons you were. It was a colorful story. Many houses still standing in this area were built by David Babson for his children.

This house was built in 1874. You can still see some remnants of the Federal period around here . . . little eyebrows over the windows, you see some little peaks over the windows inside, reminding one of Federal architecture. You can see some vestiges of Victorian influence here and there also and even a little gingerbread on the outside. It is an early Gothic carpentry house.

There was a community wide sense of responsibility toward all the children in town when I was growing up. When we brought home a report card that said we were "inclined toward mischief" under the deportment heading we were in deep trouble. We'd be told that if we thought we had trouble with our teacher we hadn't seen anything to match how deeply we were in trouble at home. Our parents had an ingrained sense of respect for authority and this was passed on to us in no uncertain terms. We were not in school to fight with the teacher. You respected whichever teacher or adult corrected you. And we all respected anyone who had been smart and lucky enough to have formal education beyond high school: we respected learning.

Having two older brothers I learned diplomacy at an early age. Both boys loved

repairing old cars known as "junks" and this became the bane of my father's existence for a while, my father being a compulsively neat man who kept his place like a park. For several years there were always one or two old cars in our orchard with the boys working on their respective "great finds." One particular car was a Willys Knight touring car and it had room for six or seven people, all friends of my brother. On summer evening these guys would all pile into the car and head off for Gloucester. For years I thought the Willys Knight car was the Willys Night car, so named for their nocturnal jaunts to the "city". (In local parlance we called Gloucester "the City" and Boston "the Big City")

Some of this same group of boys, on another summer evening, found several gallons of home-distilled whiskey tucked in amongst the rocks down in Folly Cove, waiting to be picked up by bootleggers. Making whiskey was one of our cottage industries at the time. I remember being awakened by sounds of mysterious actions as a couple of strapping lads hauled one of my inebriated brothers up the back stairs under the careful direction of an older sister. I yelled in a loud voice, "Why has he peed himself?" and this query woke my mother. She proceeded to admonish them and gave an impromptu lecture on the evils of drinking unknown whiskey and listed the perils of ingesting wood alcohol and methanol instead of good grain alcohol. This may well have started my interest in chemistry, which interest later blossomed into medicine.

During the summers of our youth we all had chores to accomplish before we could play. These chores were divided into activities appropriate to our age and sex and had to be performed to our parents' satisfaction. Swimming was the most memorable and most active of our summer frolics. One summer day at the Babson pit, as we stopped off for our usual rinse off of salt water, stands out in my memory as the day a group of us girls became upset because a certain Mr. Shapiro, who had bought the cottage next to our house at the end of Gott Avenue, brought a group of his friends to the pit for a swim and one of them was naked.

In those days girls were more modest than they seem today and didn't usually swim naked. We girls reluctantly and with much grumbling went on our way past the pit and met Lottie Pratt Parady who was out for a walk. We told her of our dismay at what we'd found at the quarry and she indignantly strode to the quarry's edge and aggressively told the Shapiro party to leave the area. Mr. Shapiro announced authoratively that his naked guest was a Doctor Gregory Pincus of Clark University, who was about to become reknowned for his research on a pill which would someday control the entire population of the world. To which Lottie replied, in all her Yankee firmness, "Doctor Pink Ass or Doctor Red Ass better get out of here or I'll call the law!"

Shortly after that we regained our favorite swimming spot. Many years later that very Doctor Pincus became famous as the father of the birth control pill.

In Pigeon Cove (*the North Village*) we had our own history which was sometimes a bit unlike that of the South Village, Rockport. We had the Scandinavians around Pigeon Hill and Italians in the northerly sector of the North Village but we were not really restricted or isolated from each other.

One great thing about growing up here was that you played with kids of all kinds of different nationalities and everyone got along. When I see all the focus on singular ethnicity I wonder that more people don't assimilate as they once did. You came to this country and you tried to get along with everyone. Here on Cape Ann you have the Scandanavians, Irish, Italian, Portuguese and we all managed to get along as Americans. Our parents and grandparents were all determined to become Americans. They would never have even thought of introducing a second language into the school systems. People kept their ethnicity within their families but made no public demands for others to accept it.

View of an unpaved and shopless Bearskin Neck with the twin spires of the Congregational and Universalist churches looming in the distance.

JAMES RAYMOND SMITH

Born in Rockport in 1888, died in December, 1947. Founder and proprietor of the J. Raymond Smith lumber yard, and later the L. E. Smith hardware stores. A leading citizen of the town for many years, known for his well developed sense of civic responsibility and local philanthropy. This entry has been taken from Smith's own handwritten journal, which was meant for his children and grandchildren. I have received gracious permission from his son Ray and his grandson Jay to include these excerpts from a rare glimpse into the life and times of a very well known Rockporter.

I WAS BORN IN Rockport, Massachusetts in a house on Holbrook Court. My father was Austin Clifford Smith and my mother was Ann Hartzhorn (Hale). She was born in Pigeon Cove in 1860. She died when I was about 4 1/2 years old. About a year after that my father married Ellen Haraden of Lanesville. My stepmother was a very fine woman and did for us children as much as any mother could do for her own.

Most of my life was spent in the South End of Rockport. I remember Long Beach when the electric cars from Gloucester ran down to the edge of the beach to an open-air theater where they had plays in the summer evenings and band concerts in the afternoons. There was no road from Rockport but the street railway tried very hard to get passengers to go to Long Beach from Gloucester and had barkers to meet the excursion boat from Boston and tell the passengers of the wonderful shore dinners to be had at Long Beach. There was a merry-go-round, dance pavilion, tintype photographer and all the inducements (on a smaller scale) such as were seen at Coney Island and Revere Beach. There was no sea wall except some wooden piers driven in the sand and perhaps how and then some bulkheads that supported a plank walk and 25 or 30 summer cottages built up on wooden posts.

At Saratoga (a salt water creek that still goes into the marsh behind the Long Beach cottages) we boys used to go swimming and sailing on rafts over the marshes when the tide was high. The first house after leaving Long Beach was Christopher's on the marsh at the end of the path that came through the woods from Rockport. It was near here (at the end of Pebble Beach) that the trans-Atlantic Cable ran to Canso, Nova Scotia. From here a cable ran underground to the Cable House in Rockport (on Norwood Avenue) where the messages were relayed overland on wires to Boston and New York.

As a boy I helped my father on the farm and became more or less familiar with the woods and land that my folks owned. I drove a milk team one summer in the evenings, delivering milk to the summer colony at the South End of town. At one time I had a small milk route of my own, using my father's horse and buying the milk from him. At that time the retail price for milk was seven cents a quart. I paid my father five cents a quart and sold it for seven cents. There were no milk bottles back then: we measured out the milk with a metal measure and poured it into the customer's pitcher.

I remember one customer that I had who only wanted 1/2 pint of milk each day. I would measure it out in my quart measure and carry it up to her back door which was at least 100 feet from the street and pour it into her measure. On the second day she would pay or leave in a cup three cents and on the fourth day leave four cents. There was no bookeeping but I could figure it took a lot of work to earn two cents.

I went to the first four grades of school in the Cove Hill School (which used to be the Boy Scout Hall). I went to the fifth grade in a room in the Town Hall and the sixth, seventh and eighth grades in the old Broadway School (torn down to make space for the present police-fire stations). I went to one year of high school in the old high school which was in what is now the Community House, next to the Catholic church on Broadway.

I remember in those days a big steel tramp steamship, the Wilster, loaded with sugar, came ashore in the fog on Long Beach. Her crew was taken off in a breeches buoy by the Coastguardsmen, or as we called them, the Life Saving Crew. My father used his horse to haul their equipment to the beach. The first person to come ashore was the cabin boy, more drowned than alive, and some tried to give him some whiskey but he would not take it as he had promised his mother never to drink it. Most of her load of unrefined sugar was thrown overboard before she could be hauled off the beach. The farmers brought the empty sugar bags back to their farms.

There was another ship, the Hattie Page, a three masted schooner loaded with stone which came ashore on Back Beach and was a total loss there. Rockport at that time was a big producer of rough stone, used in building foundations. Many sailing ships were used to carry this stone to Boston, New York and other places. I remember the names of some of them: the Ann Parker, the Screamer, the Mary White, the Trumbull. I took several trips to Boston in the summer on the Trumbull with Captain Fred Hanson

and his son Fred, about my age.

The men who fished in small boats for lobsters and ground fish did not have power in their boats back then. They had to row with oars or sail with a small "leg of mutton" or sprit sail and many more fished out of here then than do now (1943). The isinglass industry was flourishing at that time, with three factories going in Rockport and more in Gloucester. The fishermen dried and cured fish sounds and dried fish on flakes (outdoor wooden stands) on Bearskin Neck.

The fire department was all hauled by horses in those days and when the church bells rang for fire everyone would try to get their horses hitched to the fire wagons first because the first ones there to hook up got $5.00 for that fire.

Where the High school (the present brick affordable senior housing at the foot of Broadway) and George J. Tarr school (now the Denghausen Library) stand were the stone ruins of a cotton mill with a high wooden fence around it. The Tarr school was the machine shop for the mill before it was remodeled into a school. It was raised about five feet.

When I was 15 or 16 years old I wanted to join the Navy and I left school to do that. But my father found a job for me with George W. Harvey (a Rockport boy who had gone to Boston and become a successful contractor) to learn the brick layer's trade. I started to work for him in April, 1906, and learned the trade from him for $6.00 a week for three years. I got what was called salary money, an extra $50 at the end of the first year and $60 at the end of the second year and $70 at the end of the third year. At the end of the third year I made 60 cents an hour, or $28.80 for a full weeks pay. In those days this was about the highest pay received by any of the mechanics in the building line. I was working a job in Millis when I had to come back to Rockport because my father was sick and he wanted me to come home. That ended my working away from home and I laid brick around here and in Gloucester along with some out of town work but came home every night.

I started in the ice business in about 1914 in Lanesville. I bought about 1000 tons of ice from Eugene Day every year for many years. I later bought out the Annisquam Ice Company and cut ice in a pond belonging to Miss Olga Dingard. The ice business was all right but it was an awful rush in the summertime. Help was hard to get and I used to work very hard from 5:30 in the morning until as late as 8:30 at night. I used to make as much as $3000 a year with most of the work done in about four months. But the work was too hard and as I had begun buying and selling lumber when I had time, I decided to sell the ice business when I had a chance. I got that chance and sold it in 15 minutes. After clearing up my bills I had $2000 left and I gave $1000 to my wife Mary and with the other $1000 I bought lumber.

During the time when I was in the ice business we bought the Old Tavern, where the Rockport Art Association is at present. At that time it was occupied by the Sandy Bay Club, which was in financial difficulties and wished to sell the whole thing: building and club equipment consisting of three pool tables, a lending library, a nice directors set of furniture that I sold to the Granite Savings Bank, dishes enough to serve a hundred or more people which I sold to the Spiran Lodge. I bought the place for $3200 and after running the club room as a pool room for a couple of years I sold the whole place for $4200.

The way I started in the lumber business was gradual. I bought a field on High Street one lot below and across from our house on High Street and I built a structure out of an old barn to keep my trucks in. Then I built a two story building on the same lot: the first story of brick with some room for storage so I bought a carload (railroad car) of shingles and other things in the building material line. As I was still in the ice business and calling at hundreds of houses every day, I had the opportunity to take many orders from my ice customers. This was after the first World War and prices were on the decline so I was able to buy everything on the decline and sell a little under the prices that the established dealers were trying to get.

Charles "Brud" Burbank and Burton Doloff were among my first employees and now after 20 years are still with me. From 1910 onward began the decline of horse transportation and the increased use of motorized trucks until 'long about 1925 the use of horses on the streets had almost entirely disappeared. This also meant a decline in the grain business. The D. B. Hodgkins & Son grain business in Gloucester had a smaller outlet in Rockport which they closed down to consolidate in Gloucester so I bought their building at 17 Railroad Avenue. Before all this I had formed a small trust called the Rockport Real Estate Associates, to build and sell houses but as the 1931 Depression came on we never built many. But we did buy the Hodgkins Railroad Avenue building.

In 1912 I married Mary Todd, George Todd's daughter, and we were together until 1930 when she died of a shock (probably a stroke). In 1931 I married Ellen Novak, a girl from Cambridge who had a house on

Granite Street that she had built. She was a fine girl but passed away, probably from an embolism, about seven days after giving birth to our daughter, Geneva Ann. This put quite a crimp in my ambitions and work for a while. But it is one of the wonders of life that with a little girl to look out for and live for I soon became interested again. I married Edna Louise Brannan of Worcester in 1932. She had owned and operated a summer tea room on Bearskin Neck, which she continued to do after we were married.

In 1936 I purchased the Gruening property (which became the well known Driftwood Farm) in the South End and we went to live there that winter. This was a big 21 room house and about 14 acres of land. We started to keep summer boarders as soon as we could and were quite busy during the summer months. I plowed and planted quite a lot of land and that kept me busy most of my spare time. I had help before the war but not much during the war (World War II). In 1936 I also bought the Hooper lumber yard next to the railroad depot off Railroad Avenue from Norman and Harry Hooper.

I don't think we have any soldier heroes in our family, at least any that I've run into in our family history. But I do think I should write about Elmer Smith, whose life would be an example of grit and courage to anyone. Elmer Smith was the son of William, son of Solomon the first, who was son of Joseph, who was my great, great grandfather.

He grew up in Rockport like any normal boy to young manhood, when he developed some disease of the bone and his arm had to be amputated above the elbow. After this surgery he went to Boston to work where he drove a laundry wagon in Cambridge and was married. He found competition quite keen and the work quite hard so he came back to Rockport and started a business here: a laundry route.

But his bone trouble was still with him and they were obliged to amputate one foot and then all the way up to his hip. Between the times he was not being cut up he still tried to do business. He was in the insurance business for a while. In the course of years he lost his wife (by death) and he had his other foot cut off and then his other leg at the hip. He lost three fingers of his left hand and had only a thumb and finger on that hand and a stub on his right arm.

He was always cheerful and it was an inspiration to visit him and hear him enthuse about plans he would like to carry out. At about this time he sent for me one day and told me that most of his money was gone, but that he owned the house he lived in. The first floor was let and he lived on the second floor with a family who took care of him; the rent helped to pay for their services. He had a big back yard and he wanted to build a small house there with what money he had so that he could get a little more income. He wanted me to help him with advice and material as as I was just then starting in the lumber business.

I did what I could for him. Tied into a chair looking out of his back window he supervised and planned the building of a small house in the back yard and so well did he do the job, and so cheaply, that several people wanted him to supervise similar houses in other parts of town but the doctors found it necessary to operate once again: on his stomach this time and that killed him. Most of all this time he was in great pain but he was always cheerful and would not give up. Although his life seemed hopeless he kept up his courage and to me was a hero.

My great grandfather was named Joseph

and it was he who owned and left to his children a strip of land starting at Straitsmouth (Gap) about 40 rods (660 feet) wide and running straight back on a south line 500 or more rods (8250 feet) after it crossed the road at the old poor farm (the present DenMar). A stone wall enclosed this land except for about 100 (1650 feet) rods more into the South Woods. My father was a farmer and farmed the same land his father, grandfather and great grandfather had before him. My grandmother Hannah Poole Smith was the daughter of Aaron Poole whose farm was the next big farm going south from the Smith farm. What is now Country Club Road was the Smith Lane into the woods and the next one was the Poole's.

I am told that practically all the land below the Turks Head Inn was once the land of Asa Todd and it was his home that formed a part of the Inn. A caretaker, Robert Tarr, lived there all winter. A boardwalk used to run all the way from the Inn to the beach. The next buildings toward town from the Inn were, as I remember it, two stables: one owned by Tim Sheahan and the other by Harvey Tarr. Going along toward town the next house was Johnny Grover's, on the corner of what is now Eden Road. The land along Eden Road was opened up and roads built by a man named Reynolds: he built the large house on the point (torn down and replaced) which he called Paradise Cliff.

The next house was around the corner where the late Mr. Stratton once lived. A man named Frost (we called him Monkey Frost) lived there. He was a farmer and I know of one field he planted in what is now the Southern Woods and is all grown over with trees.

The next house was that of Aaron Poole. He was my great-grandfather and his brother, Story Poole, lived in a house nearby. Along here on the shore your maps will show Whale Cove. We always called it Aaron Poole's Cove but I do remember a whale coming ashore a little further along between this cove and Reynold's Point. We boys walked all over the whale and I now have the backbone of that whale. It took years of sun and weather to bleach the oil out of it. Story Poole started what is (was) now the Cape Ann Tool Company. Both houses were moved away and are now on Briarstone Road.

The next place along South Street was the house owned by a man named Brooks which became Saint Ann's summer camp for children. After that came what is now the Rockport Lodge which was part of the estate of two brothers, David and Solomon Smith. The barn across the street (still standing and part of the Lodge) was divided into two parts and each brother kept his horses and cows in his side. This land was a part of the estate of Joseph Smith and it ran to the water toward the east and westerly almost to Gloucester. What is now Country Club Lane was the wagon track that Smith used to get to his farm and woodland.

Along that same side of the street came the Town Poor Farm opposite the home of Robert Tarr. Then came Smith, Gott and Andrew Lane. The first houses on Marmion Way as I recall, were Mosley's, Dillaway, Sandborn and L.E. Smith, whose house was built on what is now called Pioneer Circle.

At the end of Marmion Way is Gap Cove, between Straitsmouth Island and Gap Head on the mainland. After a severe winter storm large quantities of rockweed could be found along the shore of this cove. The farmers were very industrious in hauling it off to put on their fields for fertilizer. I have two agreements signed by the Smith and Gott families, dividing the week into days that each family could haul rockweed, binding themselves in the sum of $500 not to haul except on the days agreed upon. Each offense required the offender to pay $50 to the other party.*

Then came Frank Choate and next to him was Jim Bradley. Mr. Bradley and Jessie Savage made up the whole Rockport police department. As I remember him Bradley was an old man with a cane and a constable's badge but he kept the townspeople within the law as well as as does today's police department. Mr. Bradley had a large fruit orchard with grape vines, apple, plum and cherry trees. And very nice fruit it was. We boys were no respecters of private property and found his orchard as easy to raid as anyone elses. Now that I think of it, it seems that there were a great many nice tasting and rare early fruit in the orchards fifty years ago that cannot be found in Rockport today. It seemed as though everyone had at least one or two very nice fruit trees in their yard.**

Fred Gott on Gott Street kept a barn full of cows which would not be appreciated today. What is now Atlantic Avenue was called Bay View Street years ago. There were no houses on the water side except a few fish houses and a couple of coal sheds. As you went along toward the Headlands and up to Clark Avenue there were quite a few houses but on top of the hill where the main parts of the Headlands is was all one big pasture.

This was later bought and roads opened up by a man named Jason Jiles.

On Clark Avenue there was a long house that had formerly been a bowling alley and later cut up into small tenements. This was still later made into two houses and moved onto the Headlands by Mr. Jiles. One has been torn down but one still stands.

On the corner of Prospect Street and South Street lived Walter Peckham, father of George Peckham who lives there now (1940's). Then came Joe Pool, a farmer with two barns across the street. And then William Wheeler, father of Homer Wheeler who lives in the same house. Next was a house occupied by two bachelors, Bill and Tommy and their old maid sister, by the name of Bardon. Bell, the sister, had a small store in the basement and sold penny candy, knick-knacks and some groceries. We boys used to take eggs up and swap them for candy.

Going along South Street we came to a house called the Benjamin Tarr house which was occupied at the time by George Legaller. He wore a black shawl over his shoulders, had a speech impediment and had a beautiful flower garden with red poppies in front of the house. Further along was Solomon Smith's place: there was a red gate between his place and ours: ours being where I grew up from the time I was five years old. This was the entrance to what is now Caleb's Lane. It was called Caleb's Lane because it was the right of way to land owned by Caleb Pool. It was the only right of way at that

---

*In our deed here at 29 Penryn Way we note that a "seaweed right of way" extends along one boundary of our land, entitling neighbors to use this rough path to gather seaweed from the beaches.

** I remember growing up at 109 Main Street where we had a small orchard in our back yard featuring two pear trees, one red Delicious and one MacIntosh apple tree, a plum tree and grape arbor. A not uncommon sight in town in the '20's and '30's.

time to get to Caleb's beach or what is now called Old Garden Beach.

Zebulon Parsons lived in the Salt Box House along South Street from there and the house in back was occupied by Mike Knowlton. When my father would catch a woodchuck in the field he would take it to Mike to eat. He considered woodchuck a great delicacy. 7 South Street was occupied by four families and the next place, the Arnold place, belonged to Laura Young, an old maid, who one day during her visit to our house we kids had a squabble and she told my mother that she had a hard row to hoe.

On the corner of Prospect Street and South Street opposite the Peckhams in what was called the Tarr house (or Job Lane house*) and was home to a Mr. Dow. But when I was a boy it was occupied by a family named Swett.

At the end of this Smith journal I found a copy of a typewritten letter dated January 8, 1948 from one Doctor Reginald Smithwick from Boston in which Smith is advised to see the doctor on January 15 for medical tests. A terse handwritten note at the bottom reads "Came too late!" James Raymond Smith had died on December 27, 1947.

---

*This grand old small house has recently been restored by Mr. Rudolph Colao and is so much more pleasant to look at now than the vine encrusted, dilapidated structure that it had become over the years.

The Whales Jaw, a rock arrangement on Dogtown. This relationship has been forever changed now with the smaller or lower jaw no longer in this position. The graffiti shows that this art form is not new to our times.

"GOR SVENSON"

Pseudonym for a Rockport Swedish lobsterman and quarryman; such anonymity insisted upon by the "informant." This interview came to light as I was surfing the Library of Congress on the Internet, seeking any information they might have in their records about Rockport. To my amazement they not only have some photographs of old Rockport but in the American Memory archive section, American Life Histories: Manuscripts from the Federal Writers' Project: a WPA (Works Progress Administration) 1936-1940 project I found the following interviews with a Swedish-born Rockport quarryman and lobsterman, "Gor Svenson". There were at least seven separate interviews taken down in 1938-39.

As near as I can tell from the accompanying information these interviews were written down by Cape Ann resident Harry Wheeler from Svenson in Rockport over the course of some time. The original descriptions in the Library of Congress files, being fastidious bureaucratic reproductions of Wheeler's handwritten record, contain all kinds of parenthetically noted insertions which I have deleted in my attempts to make the interviews more readable. Harry Wheeler was the late husband of Erma Allen Wheeler, a Cape Ann artist of note who, at this writing is still living on Cape Ann and producing a body of remarkable paintings which display highly original interpretations of the local landscape.

At the beginning of what was a series of meetings (begun in December, 1938) between Wheeler and his subject are Wheeler's following introductory remarks:

"A RECORD OF A SERIES of interviews with a Swedish-born American who was for most of his adult years a quarry-worker in Gloucester (Bay View and Lanesville) and Rockport, Massachusetts and who is now engaged in lobstering. The thoughts, opinions, reminiscences are always those of the informant. The word-pattern is as far as possible also his. No attempt has been made to record the Scandian dialect. The full effect of the informant's virgin prose can be achieved however by reciting the material in muffled somewhat petulant tones while sitting on the end of a teeter-board in a driving rainstorm.

Gor Svenson, age 62, tall stooped, addled and harassed. High boots, corduroy trousers, lumberman's shirt, one gallus. The interviews reported were conducted in the kitchen of the informant's home, a two-story frame building rented at fifteen dollars a month, heated by three wood-stoves, lit by kerosene lamps and watered by a well seventy-five feet away. There were no storm windows and one ten by eight inch pane of glass was missing from a window which over-looks the small plot of land where would be the informant's vegetable garden if he thought a garden worth-while, which he doesn't. Stuffed into the gaping hole were a dozen copies of the Gloucester Daily Times, a local organ of enlightenment.

Under the kitchen table is a new pane of glass which the informant will doubtless insert in the window when he gets around to it, which will not be soon. The stove is warm and very noisy. On it was invariably an old fashioned coffee pot. From it coffee was constantly being poured. Sometimes the supply of liquid got low and more water was added. Sometimes the brew was a little thin, and more coffee was tossed in. The stuff was served with evaporated milk and tasted like the devil. On a good many of the visits there were several cans of beer on the table. The beer tasted very good.

Present from time to time as the interviews proceeded were the informant's widowed sister, late-fiftyish, happy, busy, and voluble, the informant's unemployed nephew, mid-thirtyish, morose, lethargic and frequently witty, and the informant's five cats to none of which the field-worker took a fancy.

This material is vitally factual. It's publication, accompanied by any identification of the informant, would unquestionably injure him socially and economically. If pressed both the informant and the field-worker will deny ever having heard of each other."

End of quote from Wheeler's opening notes. "Gor" told many fascinating stories about his early days at sea on a full-rigged sailing vessel and some of the adventures he experienced in ports all over the world, which I have opted to leave out of the current narrative. After the following brief reference to earlier days I have concentrated upon the informant's Cape Ann reminiscences in order to keep his entry in line with the local focus of the book. The rest of the text will be in "Svenson's" own responses to Wheeler's proddings.

I was young once (in Sweden). My father say, "You work hard, Gor, here on farm with me and brother. When I get old, brother get farm, but we give some land to you. Build house, build barn, everything all right!" All right, sure.

Not for me! That was near Halsingborg, my father's farm. Halsingborg big city, ten times big as Gloucester, bigger than Salem and Lynn all at once, almost thirty thousand people. I go to Halsingborg, I and other feller, work next farm. We look for work there. You work for father long time get something. Right now get work and lotta hell. Work somebody else. But we get work in Halsingborg, other feller and me: I'm fifteen then, he's maybe seventeen. We stay there two, three weeks, other feller go home, I go to Stockholm, two, three weeks, there nothing too. I have good time there, though. Good people. "Give me something to eat?" "Sure. Come home with me, we feed you, give you some pennies." Then I get job. All of a sudden I get job on ship. Big ship. Six-masted ship for Hamburg. And that was funny thing, too. You look at map some time, see Atlantic ocean. Big, huh? See what they call Baltic Ocean. Not so big, huh? Like puddle. But ask anybody. Much worse storms in little Baltic Ocean.

That Captain! He Swede-feller, strong, yellow beard. He laughed at storm. He like me, too. "Gor," he said, "you are smart boy. You learn quick and work hard. Sailing is the best thing in the world for man to do, and Swede-feller best sailor in all the world. You stay on ship. I think we go on big trip, two, three year. When we get back Sweden maybe you Captain too.!" (At this point I jump ahead in the written interview to Cape Ann information after Gor described his various adventures in seaports all over the world) I go down to water-front (in New York City) and meet Swede feller. He says "You got any money, harr?" I say I got a little money. Swede feller say, "You come to me to that Rockport place, harr, there is plenty job in the quarry. So I come.

By gosh, you should been here last night! There was big fight over Curtis Street, two three o'clock morning. So much noise you think they hear all over Pigeon Cove, all over Cape. So much noise you think maybe John Spates, Jimmy Quinn come throw them all Salem jail rest of life! Shout, swear, throw rocks, throw bottles, throw kerosene lamp, wonder no set fire to place. Bunch fellers got place over Pine Pit, stone house made from grout (the most worthless of the granite: field worker). The boys make, the young boys make for play house, but the big fellers take, hang around, play cards, drink, fight, sometime maybe take girl there, I don't know. But last night they have big fight. They play cards and one feller he don't like way other feller play, so first those two fellers fight, then pretty soon all the fellers fight. Big noise, I tell you! Make me think of days I first come to Rockport.

I first come to Rockport almost forty years gone. Much drink then, fight. Most Americans work quarries then, some Irish, then lots Swede fellers come, some Finns, some Italians. Some Swede fellers like me speak good English, been this country long time, been New York, been Boston. Some Swede fellers speak no English, they get off train Rockport all alone, sometime know somebody, got brother, got cousin, got feller same town, next farm maybe. Sometime know nobody, got sign tied on, like on fish, say "Rockport Granite Company, Rockport, Massachusetts." Some these fellers work hard, learn English quick, make friends. Other those fellers not so good job, not learn English very good, sad, nobody like. Drink a lot, those fellers.

I first come to Rockport with other Swede feller from New York. We speak English smart, got little money, go Swede woman's boarding house down Forest Street. Come in town one day, get drunk that night, celebrate, go Rockport Granite Company office, say, "We want job, harr?" Boss say,

"Go to work." Start right in. We work seven to twelve morning, one to six afternoon. First they put me work load paving on barge. Lot business paving then. Send paving everywhere in world then. Rockport Granite Company get whole lot that business, too. They pay me twelve dollars week I first go work there. Second day I work feller come around and say, "You join union, harr?" I say, "I don't know." But other Swede feller come with me say, "Sure he join union, I join union, too."

So I join union. I belong union all time I work Rockport Granite Company. After big strike no more Rockport Granite company. I still belong union, work other companies, Bay View, Lanesville. Still got my book. Maybe tomorrow feller come me say, "Hey Gor, got job for you. Six months job quarry. Good pay. Good boss. No union." I tell him go hell. All old Swede quarry fellers tell him go hell. Finn fellers either. Anybody cut stone Cape Ann can't have scab job, can't go round say, "You work, He work. Other feller work." Got go union. I belong stone cutters union. Paving cutters union got national office down in Rockport. Sometimes stone-cutters say, "Hey, that's my job." Paving cutters say, "Hey, that's my job." Have strike. Not union against boss. Union against union. No good.

Funny thing, quarry-workers all union men. Fellers work down Tool Company— sons quarry workers, lots them, brothers maybe, no union. Work like hell. In summer hot in front those forgers. In winter still hot, outside cold. Get hurt quick, either. Lots fellers down Tool Company lose fingers in forge. Finn feller over in Lanesville used come round now sell Daily Worker, he lost three, four fingers in hammer come down. I would not want work there. Make tools all kinds bit tools. Make wheels I don't know what for. Make parts airplane factory. Some fellers may make thing go round that Lindbergh plane first time down there. Dean fellers run Tool Company. Brothers. Lindley Dean one brother. Sail boat races. Other brother live Magnolia. You know feller told me? Feller told me that Dean feller brother got wife she die in bath tub. What he do? Make gold bath tub. Still got! I don't know.

I am in Rockport no more six months I get married Lutheran Church young Swede girl come over here get job. She pretty, that wife, but no good for wife. I like lots boys, girls. She like no boys, girls all. I come home one night she gone. Feller say she go off with fisherman over Gloucester. I don't know. All right she don't come back. One time nine, ten years after, I drink beer in Gloucester feller say to me, "See that feller, Gor? That feller over there run off your wife." I look at that feller. He look at me. We don't say nothing, harr!

After that wife go my sister, her husband come over from old country live with me. They got two boys. When they come got one boy, Nels. Pretty soon got another boy, Henry. That husband my sister nice feller. Quiet, no fight, no drink. Just smoke, give my sister all his money. Very happy that husband my sister. Feller say to him, "Hey, you think you ever go back?" (to Sweden) He say, Sure. When they build bridge! Very funny.

He paving-cutter. Good paving-cutter. Paving-cutter should wear mask. Paving-cutter doesn't wear mask. Company got. Lot dust. Stone dust. Got consumption. Company got masks, but paving-cutter don't wear. That husband my sister can't work. Spit blood. Give up job paving-cutter. Just quarry worker like me. Can't do that, too.

Go home. Go doctor. No good. Die. Reason paving-cutter don't like mask, don't like feel, can't do so much work. Piece work paving cutting.

Quarries full of water now, derricks pull down they do not fall, kill somebody, tracks off Japan make cannon, barges rot, docks like paper. Quarry fellers forget how be quarry-fellers. Some could not hold drill now, hit with hammer. Would not know what. You tell me that when I come Rockport I laugh! You tell me that back big strike I laugh. We had big strike back 1925, everybody go out, company won't pay union scale.

Won't go back but get union scale. How long you think strike last, harr! That right. Quarry fellers don't go back Rockport Granite Company quarry one year. Little while get strike benefit, then no. Union no money. Some fellers while strike go work some place else. Few work scab wages some place else. Most don't do nothing. Company try run quarry with Italians and guards. Cannot do it, no. Italians don't cut enough stone to drown cat. They put them in house near Peter Bernard's garage. (the former Cheshire Cat antique store at 105 Granite Street, across from Burbank Auto, now condominiums) Some nights strikers throw stones at house, do not want hurt, just scare.

Bimeby company settle, union win, but one year long time be on strike. The company some feller tell me, lose million dollars try break that strike. After that quarries do not work long. Cut stone entrances big tunnel New York and big bridge down Rhode Island. Pretty soon close. I guess those Rogers fellers spend too much time Country Club, not enough time quarry. Year long time strike.

When Rockport Granite Company close up I think not for long. Business bad.

Pretty soon business good. Old wood building wear out, old wood bridges fall down, somebody die, got have statue. I think maybe Rogers brothers not such good business men. Maybe some other business man come Rockport, buy quarries, give everybody job. Not yet. Feller come now, got buy pumps, put up derricks, lay tracks, build shops, get barges, machines, tools. Got get men, too. Lot quarry men here you think, harr? Lot used-be quarry men! Like me.

I got little work now then after company close up. I work Leonard Johnson's little while. I work little while Fitzgibbon's over Lanesville. There was work two three years ago some fellers. Build breakwater Newburyport, got have stone. No job for me.

No more quarry work I guess fifteen, twenty years. Then work. Much work then, harr! Then all buildings, bridges, roads made last ten, fifteen years go pieces. You see. Everybody see. Stucco no good, concrete no good, only granite good. Everybody want granite then. Nobody want something else ever some more. Quarries open again.

Quarries stay open, harr! Everybody got job! Quarry job!

One time (1932) somebody kill Swede tailor feller* over on Main Street, Rockport. Right in day-time too. Everybody say that Cregg he get murderer. They say he could not put Jesse Costello in jail and everybody sore. He better catch these murder all right, or he lost job. But he don't catch murderer. And he don't lose job, too! Maybe, Gor, you could catch murderer. Maybe, you have some police, some money, you go around ask questions, write down what they say, maybe you find out, get a lot of money, maybe they make you G-man. I got pretty good guess who kill Swede, anyway. I think maybe Finn people do it. Finn people do not like Swede fellers. I know some Finn fellers they are all right. Some my friends they Finn fellers. But they do not like Swedes. Swedes bigger, smarter.

The morning after the next Halloween (following the Oker murder) I come in maybe eleven o'clock when I sell my lobsters Howard Hodgkins that feller says Hey Gor, you hear what happen, somebody kill Swede woman down Pigeon Hill Street? Feller tell me all about it. Somebody goes in that Swede woman's house kill her set fire to house! That was fire alarm I hear out in harbor. Hey, we have lot of noise after that. They get army down here, get whole American army. They come around every house, those soldiers and police, too. Fellers come from newspapers, too. Every day all over papers, "Murder in Rockport!" Everybody say he know who did it. In papers it tells police ask questions . . . they ask me questions too. Sure. They ask everybody in Rockport questions. They come right in house, look everywhere, say, Who are you? Where were you that night? Who you think kill that woman, harr? But they do not get feller that kill that woman.

One time I visit feller in Rockport and hear fire whistle. Go outdoors. Do not need count whistle. Can see fire. Big fire. Down behind cemetery behind beach. (at the Mill Pond) Old factory. Old isinglass factory. (the

*Arthur F. Oker, the author's grandfather, who was a Finnish Gypsy but whose wife, Ida, was Swedish. The murderer has never been found. The most difficult thing for the police (after the State police pulled the fingerprints of the entire Rockport police force at the crime scene) was an inability to establish a motive. Oker was well respected and patronized by the whole town.

closed up Haskins isinglass factory) Burn like hell. Too much for Rockport firemen. Some feller send Gloucester more firemen. You know how long take Gloucester firemen get over here, harr? Take only five minutes. Stop any someone's car try to go Gloucester from loop, say. No. Go Long Beach. Stop car try go Rockport up hill near garage. Say. No. Go East Gloucester, Brier Neck. No cars at all. Fire engines have whole road himself. Only take five minutes.

One time in Gloucester feller stop car, ask me where is post-office. I tell him I don't know. I know where old post-office is but old post-office no more post-office. I walk up Main Street by waiting staion, I stop feller, say Where is that new post-office? Feller say, up behind City Hall. I go take look. That's big building that post-office. That's fine building. When I look at it I get sick almost my stomach. I tell you why: that's granite building. Good granite building. Rockport granite. Come from Leonard Johnson's quarry over Pigeon Cove. Leonard Johnson Swede feller. Come from Sweden poor feller just like me. Work in quarry save money, get own quarry. But that is not why I get sick almost to my stomach. How far Providence, harr! Eighty miles Providence, harr? All right. How far new post-office from Leonard Johnson's quarry, harr? Five miles. All right, either.

In Leonard Johnson's quarry they cut stone. Good stone. But do they finish stone at that quarry? No, by gosh! They take that good stone, ship on Peter Bernard's trucks all way Providence, finish stone Providence, bring back to Gloucester! Every stone go into post-office get nice ride to Providence, nice ride back! You think that is right? You

think that is what they should do, harr? It makes me sick almost to my stomach!

Two three weeks ago lots Swede quarry-fellers all excited. Used be quarry-fellers, I mean. Now lobster fellers like me, fish fellers, WPA fellers. They go round every-where, say, You know what that Bates* tell that Congress? He tell that Congress get a lot of money, send to Rockport, finish break-water! Three, four hundred fellers get job two, three years, take out stone, make Rockport breakwater all done, make Rockport harbor best harbor world. Big enough whole United States Navy now. I see whole United State Navy Rockport harbor five six times. Could get Swede navy in that harbor too. But not in storm. Storm come up, most from northeast, blow United States Navy, Swede Navy all over Beach Street. If they finish breakwater, though, storm could not blow nothing.

Those Swede quarry fellers all excited. All excited but me. I say, What the hell? What you care, harr? Even if Congress give that Bates that money finish that breakwater no jobs you me. Jobs Providence! Well, Congress do not give that Bates that money anyway. I do not know why. One feller, Finn feller say think maybe fix up harbor all right for United States Navy.

You know that bridge down by Rockport Granite Company Quarry? (the keystone bridge between Rockport and Pigeon Cove) Made of granite that bridge. You gone, I gone, Hitler gone, Roosevelt gone, that bridge still be there, wait and see! Lots fine buildings made of Rockport granite. The Court up in Salem, that is fine building, that is made of Rockport granites. They got big museum in Boston near what they call

---

* Congressman William Bates, who represented this district in the national Congress for many years.

Fenway that is made of Rockport granite. Look, I show you. I got book here pictures all kind of buildings made out of Rockport stone. (Gor produces a folder listing the Houbigant Bldg., N.Y.C., Seaboard National Bank, N.Y.C., Mellon National Bank, Pittsburgh, fountains in Union Station Plaza, Washington, D.C., Longfellow Bridge, Boston-Cambridge, Eagles on the Boston Custom House, etc.) You want see good granite building some time you just go over see Gloucester Trust Company. That good Rockport granite.

One time last summer I go over Rockport Granite Company quarry, walk down on dock, see stone-cutter's sheds, all go to pieces, walk under bridge, along where tracks was, all gone down, pull up, send Japan. All railroad tracks in Rockport pull up, send to Japan. (Pre-World War II, when the United States sent thousands of tons of scrap metals to Japan, to be returned to us at Pearl Harbor.) I go by blacksmith shop, all fall to pieces, by power house, nothing there, all rot. I almost cry I tell you. When I come to Rockport four five hundred feller work that quarry, take out stone, cut stone, ship everywhere. Now nobody cut stone at all. Nobody want stone. Now cement, stucco, brick. Just use little stone now. Got to let go, got to let go to pieces, got to let rot. Almost make me cry.

I get little work now then after Company close up. I work Leonard Johnson's little while. I work little while Fitzgibbon's over Lanesville. There was work two three years ago some fellers. Build break-water Newburyport, got have stone. No job for me then. I fisherman then. Other feller me set trawls off Halibut Point get cod, get pollock, get hake. Some weeks ten make week's pay. Some make twenty five dollar.

Most week make money for gas, for bait, for paint for boat, few pennies beside. I give that up. I give feller my share fishing boat for small gas launch and skiff. I find few lobster pots, fix up, find more. Now I lobsterman for good, I guess. Not once make ten dollars week yet, half time make five, half time nothing.

I go funeral one time Swede feller don't go church. He know he die pretty soon, got cancer, leave letter. Letter say, "Don't believe church. When die don't want church. Don't want minister." I go that feller funeral. Just me, his wife, couple more fellers, undertaker. No go church first. No have minister grave. Just stand there put feller in ground like dead horse, dead dog you like. Wife cry like anything. She church woman. She want to have funeral church, have minister grave. But she have promise that feller she would have like he like, not like she like. She cry. Nobody say anything. No prayer. No speech. Just before they throw in dirt one Swede feller he cannot stand nobody say anything. He take off hat, start cry, walk edge of grave say, "Please God, we come here bury Albert. Albert good feller, God. Good workman. Good to wife. Good to fellers. You be good to him, please God." I cry, either.

Motif #1 seen from an unusual northeasterly point of view in the main harbor. Probably sometime near the turn of the century.

LARS-ERIK WIBERG

Born in 1928, Lars was not born on the Cape but has lived most of his adult life here year round and before that spent his summers mostly on Bearskin Neck. He has served his adopted town loyally and without recompense: serving on the Planning Board and the Board of Appeals for many consecutive years. He has degrees from both MIT and Harvard University and has unhesitatingly put his demonstrated intellectual expertise on the line in all of his endeavors for the town.

I WAS BORN IN WAKEFIELD. I was raised in Melrose: we were living in Melrose but it was a Wakefield family. My aunt, Anna Heurlin, spent a summer in Orange, Mass in 1925. She spoke with a friend and said she'd like to spend some time on the coast and the friend suggested Rockport, it was an interesting place. She stayed someplace on the Neck: in those days every place had a name and she met the Perretts who were living in the Oil House. That's the place on the Neck where John Chetcuti had his studio later on. That was where they used to cook fish sounds to extract the oil. When Galen Perrett built the place I now live in (*the Castle at 156 South Street*) he brought the big iron kettles they used in that process with him: we've got one of them left.

When I was about to be born my dad was ill; he had an ulcer and his doctor said he should take a month off and take it easy; he'd been trying to get a business going. I was due and I don't suppose that helped him any. So my parents rented a house on Middle Road on the Neck. I spent the first month of my life in 1928 in a wash basket in that house. My dad went down on Bradley Wharf and heard the Swedish lobstermen from Skane hollering back and forth to each other and could tell that they were from the same province in Sweden he came from: Olaf Nordling, Alfred Nelson, some of those guys. So he hollered at them in the same provincial dialect. After this he started going out with Alfred Nelson: he forgot about his diet, he ate lobsters and completely forgot his ulcer. He was as sound as a dollar in a month.

So we started to come down every summer, but we didn't always stay on the Neck. We stayed several years on North Road on the Neck and then we stayed on King Street at the Bowmans. It was a little place, wasn't the size of this room. It was right out where the Mill Brook comes down the valley there. One day my dad and I were standing next to the brook and my dad sort of sniffed the air and announced, "spent mash." Someone upstream was making booze and letting the residue go down the brook.

One summer my mother decided to rent a place over in Annisquam on Sunset Hill. That only was for one year: the next year we were back in Rockport. She missed Front Beach. In those days nobody ever swam on Back Beach. We were advised to never play where the brook came down to the beach: where the mash came from.

I remember being given a dime for a tonic at Jimmy's Sunrise. Jimmy wouldn't charge the two cents for the bottle if it was drunk on the front porch. And those brined pickles were five cents a piece.

I always gravitated toward the Neck. If you weren't at the beach the Neck was a fun place to be. When I began to strike off on my own I'd get down onto the Neck and I began to like the Pewter Shop: Lew Whitney had all that machinery to make his pewter and I was attracted to that. I'd make some simple objects from pewter and fool around with lead and the like: this was pre-World War II. This was about the time I met Ann and Pete Lindenmuth who were renting from the Maddocks in what later on was called the Sail Loft, or it could have been the Barn.

When I was a kid I used to have a recurring dream; the same damned dream, I'd have it two or three times a year. We'd get in the car and we'd take it and go to a place like Rockport. The route we took in the dream wasn't at all like the route we took to get to Rockport. When we came to Rockport each summer we used to drive through every damned town and hamlet along the way. In the dream we'd get to a place a lot like the Neck and there was a place where you turned to the right, a lot like Bradley Wharf. And that would bring us to where we had been going and the dream was over. I never made the association between that dream and the Neck, it was too tenuous.

Then just before the war started they had started building 128, they got it out into Danvers somewhere, and the war stopped that project. But we'd go to the end of 128 and then take whatever route seemed shortest. We started down through Beverly and I remember my mother saying one time that we'd go a different way. So we went a different way: it was the same way as in the dream! (I hadn't been that way for a long time until three or four years ago when I stumbled upon it and I was kind of dumbfounded at that.) Now I thought the route and the dream began to make sense. The upshot of the whole thing was clear when my aunt bought what we called the Fish

House, one place that had no Neck name; it was next door to Shorty Lesch's old fish house. She bought it in 1954, and at that point my dream stopped. I had reached my destination. Betty and I lived there for eight years before we moved into the old Perrett place on South Street, which had been the house owned by the people my aunt met when she first came here. Perrett's wife Antoinette was rather short, and when we bought the place we had to raise a lot of the stuff inside to make it comfortable for us.

I lived with my aunt in the summers and she had a shop on the Neck she rented from Otis Cook which she called the Cape Ann Craft Shop and she took stuff on consignment. Before that she and my mother had worked occasionally in the Pewter Shop. So this was like home to me.

For a long time the Neck didn't change a whole helluva lot. You could eat at the Yellow Bowl or the Driftwood or the Three Bears run by Doris Pierce. One of the more colorful characters on the Neck at that time was Aubrey "Pie" Green.

At that time a lot of people had their sewer pipes run underground right into the harbor: there were only a half dozen people living there and the tides coming and going disposed of whatever came out. Pie was one of those people. On one bitter cold morning Pie was downstairs, having breakfast with his wife Marion, and he went upstairs and went to the john and let go and it all came up in the sink: the tide had come in and frozen in the pipe. Pie said not to worry about it. He went and got some oak staves, soaked them in kerosene and stuck them in the wall around the pipe after the tide went down and lit them on fire. He said that would thaw it out and they went about their daily business.

An hour or so later there was smoke seen coming up between the Ross Candle Shop and the Boat Shop. Bearskin Neck has a lot of underground caverns beneath its surface and the wind was coming in off the water and it blew the smoke along that underground disposal pipe. Pie hollered to Marion to come look at the smoke coming up from underground thinking it was quite a laugh. But somebody rang in the fire alarm. Out comes the fire department and sprayed water all over the area and Pie went out and told them to leave it alone, that it would go out all by itself. He told them what he had done and was told to get out of the way, thinking he'd probably been boozin'. They wouldn't have anything to do with him as they slid around on the ice in the bitter cold. So Pie said to hell with them, went back in the house and watched them spraying water all over the place all afternoon. And it finally went out all by itself.

Pie showed up to work as a night watchman in Gloucester one time with an alarm clock. Pie said he told his employer, straight faced, that all nightwatchmen fall asleep now and then. He says I'm honest, when I set down to read after making my rounds, I set my alarm clock for an hour ahead, just in case I nap off. Pie said, in amazement, the guy believed me.

In those days the black-back seagulls would come to the inner harbor from Pigeon Cove to spend the winter in Rockport: come spring they'd all go home. One of the ubiquitous Neck cats had been eyeing one of these gulls. The cat leaped from a stack of lobster pots on the wharf on top of the gull. The gull took off with the cat on. If the wind had been in a certain direction the gull would have take off over the water but it was onshore that day and the cat finally slid off

over dry land. That was a strong bird.

I remember when all the lobstermen went out fishing in plain old open boats. When they got their first capstans it was a different ballgame: no more pulling the pots by hand over those rollers on the rails. The old lobstermen had hands like shoe leather from all that hand work; they were awfully tough. My dad knew the Swedes in particular. I got to know a lot of them: Olaf Nordling, Ninny Johnson, Alfred Nelson, some of them were pretty good drinkers. (I mentioned one time to a cousin of mine in Sweden that they can tax alcohol up to a certain point but then at some point you begin to make your own. He began to laugh and spoke about the north, up beyond Stockholm, where there was less sales of booze than anywhere else in Sweden but more drunks: they all made their own. It's easy stuff to make.)

We went over to Sweden when I was about five years old: we went there for a whole summer. I was walking through Kristianstad about five years ago; the first time back since I was a kid, and I felt the strangest sensation of being at home. I felt more at home there than I feel in parts of Boston. My grandfather was from there, my mother and her people were all born in the area: I don't know if it might have been something genetic about the place that made me feel that way. Our daughters were with us on the trip and Margaret looked at me in amazement and said, "Dad, you look like the people here." When I was standing outside I had someone come up to me and ask, in Swedish, what time it was and I asked her, if I told her what the time was in English would she understand me, and she was quite startled.

I can remember when the Waddell

brothers built boats on the Neck and I remember the launchings. And Oscar Waddell had a bowling alley above the shop. When the artist Otis Cook bought the place the long extension out over the road down Bradley Wharf that held the alleys was torn down. The Motif #1 hadn't been given that name when I was young: it was called wharf #1. When Eddie Wendell bought wharf #2 he renamed it Tuna Wharf. A lot of people thought that was pretty funny because they couldn't land the big tuna on Tuna Wharf, there was no derrick there. All the big tuna were landed on Bradley wharf where there was a derrick for hoisting out. I believe the artist Lester Hornby named it Motif #1. Every time Lester got a new wife, he'd build her a new house. He had a nice way about him. He was an authentic eccentric.

One thing missing from today's Neck is the Gloucester draggers that used to tie up at Bradley Wharf overnight. They'd nest up there every single night: Sebastiano and Figli, Cigar Joe, the White Owl. They were out of Gloucester but it was an awful lot more convenient for them to come into Rockport than to go all the way to Gloucester for the night and come all the way back the next day. It was not unusual to see a half dozen nested up for the night.

Ruth Spoor ran Al Hibbard's gallery on the Neck and that brought a steady influx of people who were interested in painting onto the Neck. There weren't that many artists actually on the Neck at the time: Otis Cook, Stu Urquhart, Rosenthal, Chetcuti, Tod Lindenmuth and his wife, E. B. Warren, was about all.

Now Otis Cook was a good artist and he'd knock off paintings that were essentially for the market but when he was serious he'd do some very original works. Ote got a

commission to a series of paintings for the State Street Bank one time. We all used to have burn barrels along the wharf and when your barrel got full of ashes you dumped it in the harbor and started over. I lived right down the wharf from Otie and one day I was tending my burn barrel and this guy come up to me all festooned with cameras and stuff and asked me where the artists were.

I looked over and Otis was coming out of the back of his place and I said there's one now. Otis had his suit on with a painting in each hand, probably headed for the State Street Bank. The guy looks at me and looks at Otie and I said for him to watch because he'll come out with more paintings. He came back with two more and I told the guy that he sold a lot of paintings. I had just ruined this guys stereotype of what an artist should look like: a guy in a suit stacking paintings next to his station wagon while he had been looking for a smock and a beret.

I dislike some things that have changed in Rockport since we were younger: perhaps best typified by Knowlton's Field (*a former open shore area next to Back Beach now covered with "Rowe Point" condominiums*) We could have had the field for $12,000.00 and somebody in his infinite wisdom said they could never build on that. We also had the spectacle of someone buying the old Sterling Poole estate in Dock Square, chopping a little corner of the property off and putting a knick-knack shop there. Everyone said that was a terrible thing to do. They tore down the Manning House (*a former sprawling seaside inn on Beach Street*) and put up a box of a motel. I was on the Planning Board at the time and we used that as one of the bad examples of what could happen to justify the need to rezone the entire downtown.

People need an egregious example of

what can go wrong: people fail to be able to anticipate what can go wrong and if we don't have these examples there's no telling where it's going to lead us. We needed the bad example of the motel replacement of the Manning House and chopping up the Poole property to keep motels and gift shops from springing up all over the place. We now have certain setback requirements that will prevent a recurrence of that particular problem.

I think that perhaps Doctor's Run and Boulder Top (*two large, expensive and extensive developments*) were inevitable when the sewer went in. But we have to learn to listen to people who can see areas of concern and pay attention to them before they hit us in the kisser. We have not been able to do that yet. I was with the Planning Board for six or seven years and now for the past ten years or so on the Appeal Board and I've been trying to keep the brakes on. There are others trying to do the same thing but I don't see enough concentration on these things right now.

I don't mean you've got to look for things to get in trouble over: do-gooders do that sometimes. But you've got to have somebody somewhere who can visualize a problem in the offing. You've got to keep digging away. That's the way I like to do it.

Epilogue

This book, like my others about Rockport, is not in any way intended to be anything more than a collection of communal memories being passed on to future generations by individual citizens who have generously given of their time for interviews and attention to editing details for their transcriptions. I do not pretend to have recorded all the wonderfully colorful and frequently heroic stories still lying dormant in our past. I do apologize to those who might have been willing to subject themselves to my trusty tape recorder and less than expert transcription skills, but are not included due to my diminishing energy limits.

I have not begun either of my three books about Rockport with any hope or desire to be considered a historian of any kind. I am rather the surprised recipient of these and other stories and personal histories and I feel fortunate to have been granted enough time to assemble them in what I hope are readable forms. My efforts in these undertakings have not been entered into with any hope of recompense or even local best-seller repute. These books are my gesture of thanks to the town that I once knew and continue to love: a town that nurtured me as I grew up, that continues to nurture me in my various pursuits, and has sustained me for most of my adult life. I have been so very lucky.